P9-CNG-672

Prehistoric
Animals

Prehistoric Animals

A supplement to Childcraft
The How and Why Library

1991 printing
originally published as
the 1976 Childcraft Annual

World Book, Inc.
a Scott Fetzer company

Chicago London Sydney Toronto

Copyright © 1976
World Book, Inc.
525 West Monroe Street
Chicago, Illinois 60661
All rights reserved
Printed in the United States of America
ISBN 0-7166-0666-6
Library of Congress Catalog Card No. 91-65174
B/IA

1991 printing
originally published as the 1976 Childcraft Annual

Acknowledgments

The publishers of *Childcraft—The How and Why Library*
gratefully acknowledge the courtesy of the following publisher for
permission to use copyrighted material in this volume. Full
illustration acknowledgments appear on page 298.

Page 282: Illustration from *Fantasia*, copyrighted Walt Disney
Productions. World rights reserved.

Preface

This book is a trip into the past.

It will take you back fifty million years, to a time when there were horses no bigger than dogs and fierce hunting birds taller than a man. It will carry you back to the great, green swamps of a hundred million years ago, where giant dinosaurs stalked their prey. It will show you the world of three hundred million years ago, when giant dragonflies buzzed through strange, immense forests. It will take you back six hundred million years, to a time when small, scuttling animals called trilobites lived in the sea and were the rulers of the world.

You will see wonderful events that took millions of years to happen. You will watch as the bare, lifeless land is slowly conquered—first by plants and then by many-legged animals from the sea. You'll be there as the descendants of a certain kind of fish slowly turn into the first four-footed animals. You'll see the first dinosaurs, small creatures not much bigger than a turkey. Then, before your very eyes, they'll grow into giants. And, as the dinosaurs die out, you'll see how small, furry creatures called mammals take over the world and slowly become the animals of today.

So, come take a trip into the world of the past—the exciting, wonderful, strange, and fantastic world of prehistoric animals!

**Editorial Advisory Board
for Childcraft
The How and Why
Library**

Chairman, William H. Nault, A.B., M.A., Ed.D.,
   Litt.D.
General Chairman, Editorial Advisory Boards,
World Book, Inc.

Lilian G. Katz, B.A., Ph.D.
Professor of Early Childhood Education and
   Director, ERIC Clearing House on Elementary
   and Early Childhood Education,
University of Illinois,
Urbana-Champaign

D. Keith Osborn, B.A., M.A., Ph.D.
Professor of Child Development,
University of Georgia

Kay E. Vandergrift, B.S., M.A., Ed.D.
Assistant Professor,
School of Communication, Information, and
   Library Studies,
Rutgers University

Steven Waskerwitz, M.D.
Head, General Pediatrics,
Department of Pediatrics,
Allegheny General Hospital,
Pittsburgh

Special Editorial Advisor
Alvine Belisle
École de Bibliothéconomie
Université de Montreal

**Special Consultants for
*Prehistoric Animals***

Donald Baird, Ph.D.
Director of the Museum of Natural History,
Princeton University

John Bolt, Ph.D.
Chairman and Associate Curator,
Geology Department,
Field Museum of Natural History

Peter H. Laraba (1989 printing)
Subject Matter Specialist, Geology,
Education Department,
Field Museum of Natural History

Eugene S. Richardson, Jr., Ph.D. *(dec.)*
Curator, Fossil Invertebrates,
Field Museum of Natural History

Paul Sereno, Ph.D. (1989 printing)
Assistant Professor,
Department of Anatomy,
University of Chicago

William D. Turnbull, Ph.D.
Curator Emeritus
Field Museum of Natural History

Rainer Zangerl, Ph.D.
Curator Emeritus,
Field Museum of Natural History

Contents

Learning
About the Past

Dinosaurs. Flying reptiles. Horses no bigger than dogs. These are only some of the animals that lived millions of years ago. Because all of these animals lived long before written history began, we call them prehistoric animals. The word *prehistoric* means "before written history."

Most prehistoric animals lived long, long before there were any people on earth. No human ever saw a dinosaur or a flying reptile. But, if most prehistoric animals were never seen by anyone, how do we *know* that there ever were such creatures? We know about these prehistoric animals because we have found their remains all over the world.

The outside of the earth is made up of layers of rock, like the layers of a cake. In many of the layers are the remains of animals of long ago—bones, shells, eggs, footprints, and even shapes of bodies preserved in stone.

Scientists study these remains, which are called fossils. It is from fossils that we have learned most about the animals and plants that lived on the earth in times long past.

The outside of the earth is made up of many layers of rock. The fossil remains of prehistoric animals are found in these rocks. The most ancient fossils are at the bottom.

The young fossil hunter

"Look, father, here's one!"

The little girl picked a small object out of the sand and ran to show it to the tall man. He smiled down at her, took the object, and looked at it carefully.

"Isn't it a nice one?" exclaimed the girl, hopping up and down with excitement. "It looks like the tip of a tiny cow's horn!"

The girl's name was Mary Ann Anning. She lived in England, in the town of Lyme Regis, more than 160 years ago. Lyme Regis was near the sea, and Mary Ann and her father often went to the beach. There, they hunted for fossil sea shells, or "curiosities," as people called them then.

These fossil shells looked like curled-up horns, or twisted cones, or tiny cigars. They had been buried in the cliff that towered over the beach. But wind and rain slowly pried them loose and they fell to the beach. People had many different ideas about these shells. Some people thought such objects simply grew in the rocky cliff, as a flower grows in soil. Some people thought they had been made, as part of the rocks, when the earth had been created. And some people thought they were the remains of small sea animals that had lived long, long ago.

Many people spent their summers in Lyme Regis. Mary Ann and her father sold their fossil shells to these summer visitors. Some people liked to keep collections of such things in their homes.

When Mary Ann was eleven years old, her father died. But the girl did not stop making trips to the beach to hunt for "curiosities." Many of her friends often found some of the "curiosities," too, and usually gave them to Mary Ann.

One day, her older brother, Joseph, found a very strange, large fossil skull that he gave to his sister. The skull had huge eyeholes and long, pointed jaws filled with small, sharp teeth. Mary Ann thought it must have been the skull of a crocodile. But, surely, such a thing couldn't have grown in the cliff. It must have once been a living animal!

One night when Mary Ann was nearly twelve, there was a terrible storm. The next morning, the girl hurried to the beach. She knew that the fierce wind and driving rain would have pried many chunks of rock from the side of the cliff. It would be a good day to find "curiosities."

Young Mary Ann walked carefully among all the chunks of rock that had fallen from the cliff. Then

something caught her eye. Surely, those were bones!
She began to tap at the rock with the hammer she
carried. As chunks of the rock fell away, she could
see more and more bones.

Before long, Mary Ann had uncovered the skeleton
of a strange creature! Its body was longer than Mary
Ann was tall. It had a long, crooked tail, and feet that
looked like a sea turtle's flippers. But it had no head.

Mary Ann suddenly realized that *she* had the
creature's head! The skull that Joseph had given to
her must have belonged to this strange animal!

Before long, the whole town was buzzing with news
of Mary Ann's discovery. Some workmen cut the
skeleton out of the rock. Scientists came to look at it,
and a museum bought it from Mary Ann for a large
sum of money. The young girl learned that she had

discovered a new kind of animal, an animal that had swum in the sea millions of years ago. It was given the name *Ichthyosaurus* (ihk thee uh SAWR uhs), or "fish lizard," because it was a reptile with a body shaped like a fish.

Mary Ann Anning became famous. As years went by, she became even more famous, for she found other "monsters." At the age of twenty-two she found the skeleton of another kind of sea reptile. And later, she discovered the remains of an ancient winged reptile.

Mary Ann Anning's discoveries helped people learn about the animals that had lived on earth millions of years ago. Many other people began to search for the remains of ancient animals, which became known as fossils instead of "curiosities."

Mary Ann Anning when she was a grown woman.

The stone storybook

The earth is like a storybook, filled with "pictures" of animals that lived long ago. The pages of the book are made of rock. The "pictures" are the remains of prehistoric animals buried in the rock.

The earth began to make this storybook long, long ago. Some of the first pages have been lost forever, or have not yet been discovered. But we know a great deal about the part of the story that began about six hundred million years ago.

Rivers ran through the land then, as now. And, just as now, the rushing water of the rivers tore many tiny, dust-sized bits of rock out of the land it passed through. All this wet rock dust became mud. The mud was carried along by the rivers as they moved toward the sea. Finally, where the rivers reached the sea, the mud drifted down to the sea bottom. Each year, tons and tons of more mud were added to the mud already at the bottom of the sea.

Many kinds of creatures lived in the sea. There were sponges, many-legged animals, creatures that looked somewhat like clams, and others. When these animals died, their bodies sank into the thick mud on the sea bottom. As more mud was brought by the rivers, the bodies of the animals were covered up.

Over the years, the mud grew deeper and thicker. All through the mud, from top to bottom, were the remains of dead creatures. In time, the deepest mud was packed together and turned into rock—a layer of

(continued from page 16)

rock many feet (meters) thick. And inside the rock were the remains of the dead animals.

There were different kinds of animal remains. Some were the shells of animals whose soft parts had rotted away. Sometimes, the shells were partly turned to stone. This happened when water that contained minerals—dissolved stone—seeped into tiny openings in the shells. Then the minerals hardened. Sometimes, a whole shell was turned to stone in this way. And sometimes an animal's body rotted away, leaving a hole in the mud that was the exact shape of the animal's body. Later, minerals might seep into such a hole and fill it up. When the minerals hardened, they formed a stone copy of the animal's body.

And so, the layer of rock was a page in the earth's storybook, filled with "pictures" of the animals that had lived when the rock was mud.

Day after day, for millions of years, the rivers brought more mud to the sea bottom. Day after day, for millions of years, animals died and were covered up by the mud. And, during all those millions of years, the deepest mud was always being changed into layers of rock. Each new layer of rock contained the remains—called fossils—of animals and plants that had lived and died while that layer of rock was still mud.

Many layers of this kind of rock were formed throughout earth's past. The layers are one on top of the other, like layers in a cake. The oldest layers, the ones that were made longest ago, are at or near the

(continued from page 19)

bottom. The newer layers are near the top. This means that the fossils in the lower layers are older than those in the upper layers. This is how scientists can tell which kinds of animals lived before others. Most fossils in the lower layers are much different from those in the upper layers. This shows that animals and plants have changed, or evolved, during many millions of years.

Sometimes, fossils of certain kinds of animals are found in several layers. This shows that these kinds of

animals were on earth for a long time. In later layers
there are fewer and fewer fossils of certain animals.
Finally, there are none at all because these kinds of
animals had died out.

Mud and other things that settle to the sea bottom
are called sediment. Rock formed from sediment is
called sedimentary rock. Most fossils are found in this
kind of rock. The layers of sedimentary rock, and the
fossils they contain, are the earth's stone storybook.
They tell the tale of life over millions of years.

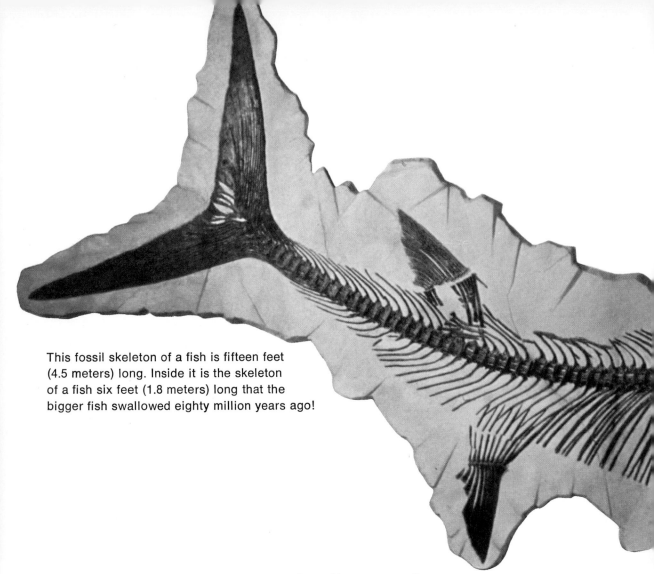

This fossil skeleton of a fish is fifteen feet (4.5 meters) long. Inside it is the skeleton of a fish six feet (1.8 meters) long that the bigger fish swallowed eighty million years ago!

Bones, shells, and eggs

Bones, teeth, shells, footprints, eggs—fossils such as these have helped us learn what prehistoric animals were like. Bones of prehistoric animals have been found in all parts of the world. Often, enough of an animal's bones have been found so that experts could put together most of its skeleton.

An animal's skeleton tells a great deal about what an animal looked like and even how it lived. The skeleton shows how big the animal was, and whether it walked on four legs or on two. Sharp teeth in the

jaws show that the animal ate meat. Blunt teeth mean
that it probably ate plants or several different kinds
of things.

Sometimes, a skeleton can even show exactly what
a prehistoric animal ate. A fossil skeleton of one big
prehistoric fish was found with the skeleton of a
smaller fish inside it! The big fish had eaten the
smaller fish.

Of course, many kinds of animals, such as worms
and insects, do not have bones. But sometimes the
shape of an animal's body was preserved in mud that
later became rock. This is how we know what many

There were once fish whose heads
were covered with hard, bony armor.
The armor of three of those fish
has been preserved in this rock.

A three-toed dinosaur made
these two footprints in mud
that later hardened into rock.

(continued from page 23)
prehistoric worms and other boneless
creatures were like. And many kinds of
animals had shells that were preserved in
rock, helping us to see what these animals
looked like.

Sometimes, an animal's skin made a
print in mud. When the mud hardened
into rock, the print was left. This is how

These children are looking at the fossil shell of an animal that lived in the sea about five hundred million years ago. Called a brachiopod, the creature looked somewhat like a clam.

This is dinosaur skin that turned to stone millions of years ago.

we know that some dinosaurs had scaly skin and that some prehistoric winged reptiles were covered with a kind of hair.

Prehistoric animals often walked on muddy ground. Sometimes, the mud hardened into rock with their footprints still in it. Such fossil footprints show us how the animals walked and ran.

Some kinds of fossils help us to see how

(continued from page 25)

prehistoric animals lived. For example, nests of fossil eggs show that dinosaurs and other prehistoric reptiles dug nests and laid eggs, just as many reptiles do now.

In addition to animal fossils, there are also many plant fossils. Prints of leaves, branches, and the bark of trees have been found. We have even discovered whole trunks of ancient trees!

Fossil plants and animals show us a great deal about the prehistoric world—even what the climate was like when these plants and animals were alive. Fossils are pieces of the past that give us a look at the animals and plants of long ago.

A small dinosaur called *Protoceratops* laid these eggs about eighty million years ago. Buried in a sandstorm, they never hatched. Minerals turned them to stone.

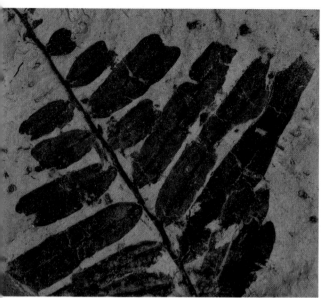

This fossil fern is eighty million years old.

This piece of fossil tree bark is three hundred million years old.

This fossil fern is three hundred million years old.

This fossil tree stump is thirty million years old.

Diatryma

Comparing animals

Scientists can tell a lot about prehistoric animals by comparing them to animals that are living now.

For example, some animals, such as the kangaroo, carry their babies in pouches. These animals have little "pouch" bones that other kinds of animals do not have. So when scientists find a fossil skeleton that also has these little bones, they know that kind of prehistoric animal carried its babies in a pouch.

Many kinds of animals that breathe air—such as walruses, dolphins, and sea turtles—spend all or most of their lives in water. These animals are all able to swim well because they have flippers instead of legs. So scientists can be sure that if a prehistoric animal had flippers, it spent most of its time in water.

Some kinds of prehistoric animals would be real mysteries if there weren't creatures like them living today. For example, there were several different kinds of prehistoric birds that couldn't fly. Their wings were too small. Scientists might have had a hard time trying to figure out how a bird that couldn't fly might have lived, because most of the birds we see can fly.

However, there are a few birds today, such as the ostrich, that can't fly. By seeing how ostriches are able to get along without being able to fly, scientists can see how the prehistoric birds that couldn't fly must have lived.

Scientists study such flightless birds as the ostrich to see how *Diatryma*, a giant flightless bird of fifty-five million years ago, may have lived.

What color was a dinosaur? Was it gray?
Or was it green? Could it have been brown
speckled with black? We don't know. This
is something we can't learn from a fossil.

What fossils can't tell us

There are many things we don't know about the
animals of long ago. There are many things that
fossils can't tell us.

Bones, footprints, or even prints of skin can't tell
us what color an animal was. We think that dinosaurs
were probably brownish or greenish, like a crocodile
or lizard. But maybe they were spotted or striped or
speckled with bright colors. We don't know.

Fossils can't tell us what kind of sound an animal
made. Did the tiny horses of long ago whinny, as
horses do today? Or did they squeak like mice or yap
like foxes? We can't tell.

We can't really be sure about the ways in which
most prehistoric creatures lived. The biggest, long-
necked dinosaurs lived on plains. Did they nibble
leaves from the tops of trees? Or did they wade
through rivers, stretching their long necks into the
water to feed on underwater plants?

Were some of the big, meat-eating dinosaurs as fierce as they seem? Or did they just eat the bodies of dead animals they found, as jackals and vultures do? We aren't sure about any of these things.

When you read about prehistoric animals, always remember that while we know a lot about them, there's a lot we *don't* know. Much of what you read about what these animals did, and most of the pictures that show what they looked like, are based on careful opinions of scientists as to what *might* have been.

The ever-changing earth

The earth is always changing. During many millions of years, mountain ranges rise and are then slowly worn down. Seas shrink away, leaving great plains. In other places, new seas appear.

Even continents change. Some two hundred million years ago there was only one huge continent. During millions of years this big continent broke up. Great masses of land moved apart to form the continents of today. And the continents are still moving.

Because the earth is always changing, fossils are often found in what seem to be strange places. Sometimes fossils of the same kind of animal are found in places that are separated by great oceans. How could these animals have gotten across the ocean? They didn't, of course. When they were alive, the two places were both part of the same huge continent—and the animals simply walked from one place to the other.

Fossils of creatures that lived and died in the sea are often found high in the mountains, thousands of miles from any sea. This is because a great mountain range may now rise where there was a seashore millions of years ago. Much of the rock that was once part of the sea bottom is now part of a mountain. And so the fossils of these animals, once buried beneath the sea, are now in the mountain.

Fossils of animals that lived in damp, swampy forests are usually found in dry, desertlike places. This is because the earth's climate has changed many times. Places that had been wet, swampy forests for millions of years dried up. In time, the mud turned to rock. The bones of forest animals, once buried in the mud, are now part of a rocky desert.

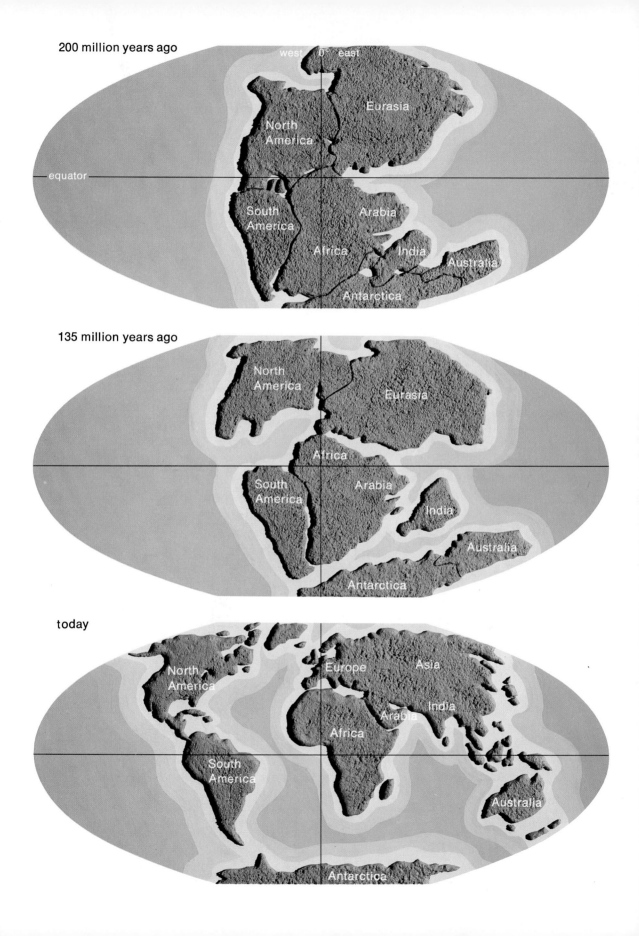

200 million years ago

west 0° east

Eurasia

North America

equator

South America

Arabia

Africa

India

Australia

Antarctica

135 million years ago

North America

Eurasia

Africa

South America

Arabia

India

Australia

Antarctica

today

North America

Europe

Asia

India

Arabia

Africa

South America

Australia

Antarctica

The "clock" in the rocks

We know that the fossils found in lower layers of rock are older than those found in upper layers. But how do we know how old fossils are? How can scientists be sure that one kind of animal lived fifty million years ago, while another kind lived five hundred million years ago?

There is a kind of wonderful "clock" in the earth's rocks. It tells scientists the age of the rocks. And once they know the age of the rocks, they know the age of the fossils buried in them.

When mud becomes rock, chemicals in the mud become part of the rock. Some of the chemicals in the rock slowly and steadily change into something else over a long, long time. Scientists have ways of measuring how much these chemicals have changed. The amount of change shows how old the rock is—when it changed from mud to rock. If scientists find that some rock is fifty million years old, they know that the fossils in the rock are also fifty million years old.

For prehistoric animals that lived in more recent times, scientists use another "clock." The bones of animals contain a chemical that begins to change when an animal dies. By measuring the amount of change in this chemical, scientists can tell almost exactly when an animal was living. But, at present, such change can be used to date back only about fifty thousand years.

A scientist carefully chips rock away from some dinosaur bones.

IF 100 MILLION YEARS EQUALED 1 YEAR

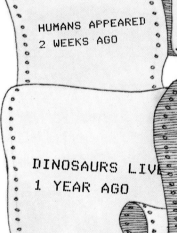

#LP:

CC

HUMANS APPEARED
2 WEEKS AGO

DINOSAURS LIV
1 YEAR AGO

How long is a million years?

Prehistoric animals lived millions, tens of millions, and hundreds of millions of years ago. But just how long a time is a million years?

Each tick-tock of a clock is one second. That's not much time. But it takes more than ten days for a million seconds to go by. If you tried to count to a million as fast as you could—without stopping to eat or sleep—it would take you about six days! And if you tried to count to a hundred million, it would take almost two years!

Scientists tell us that the earth is four billion, six hundred million years old. Another way to say this is forty-six hundred million. But no matter how you say

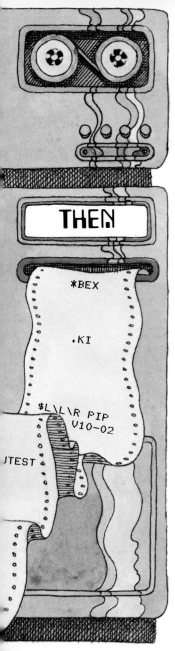

it, it is dreadfully hard to understand just how long a time this really is.

So try thinking about time in another way. Suppose you could squeeze one hundred million years into just one year—the time between two birthdays. If you think about time this way, then the earth was formed forty-six years ago. And the first living things appeared in the sea about thirty-four years ago. Five years ago, first plants, and then animals, moved onto the land. Four years ago, amphibians and then reptiles appeared. Dinosaurs ruled the earth just one year ago, but about seven months ago they all died out. Six months ago, the first horses, camels, and whales appeared.

The first humans came along about two weeks ago. Two days ago, people learned how to use fire. They invented writing only some twenty-five minutes ago. Less than three minutes ago, Columbus landed in America. And if you are nine years old, you were born just three seconds ago!

Thinking about millions of years this way may help you to understand how long ago it was that prehistoric animals lived. It may also give you an idea of how much time separated the different kinds of animals.

600 million years ago

415 million years ago

150 million years ago

Six hundred million years of life.

Fossils have given scientists a way to learn about almost all the kinds of animals that have lived on earth in the last six hundred million years. A few of these prehistoric animals, and the times when they lived, are shown here. The following sections of this book tell about these and other animals that lived at different times in the earth's past.

350 million years ago

45 million years ago

300 million years ago

1 million years ago

35,000 years ago

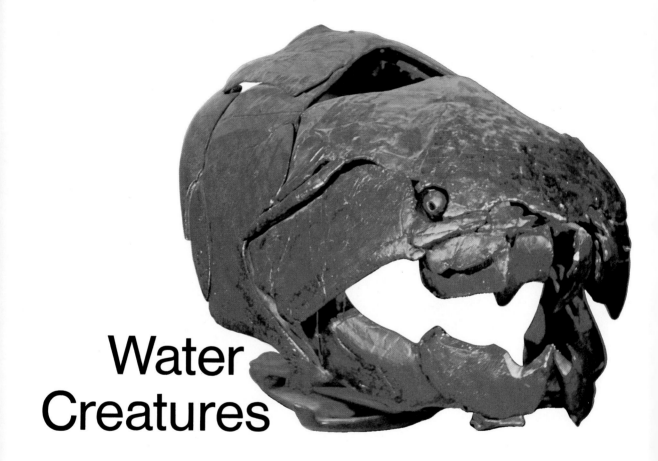

Water Creatures

The earth is very, very old. Scientists think it is nearly five billion years old.

For much of that time, the outside of the earth was just bare rock. In many places, the pointed snouts of volcanoes poked up. Out of the volcanoes came smoke, steam, and hot, melted rock from deep inside the earth.

The steam from the volcanoes cooled and turned into water. The water fell to earth as rain. After a long, long time, the rain filled in the low parts of the world to form seas and lakes.

According to scientists, life began in the sea more than three billion years ago. They think that the first living things formed out of chemicals in the warm water. For a long time, the only living things were probably tiny creatures, much like germs. Slowly, over millions of years, these tiny creatures changed and became larger, with more parts.

In time, the ancient seas were filled with many kinds of small creatures. And for hundreds of millions of years, the only animals in the world were those that lived in the water.

on the next page ▶
Five hundred million years ago, all life was in the sea. There were jellyfish, animals that looked like plants, and many-legged creatures.

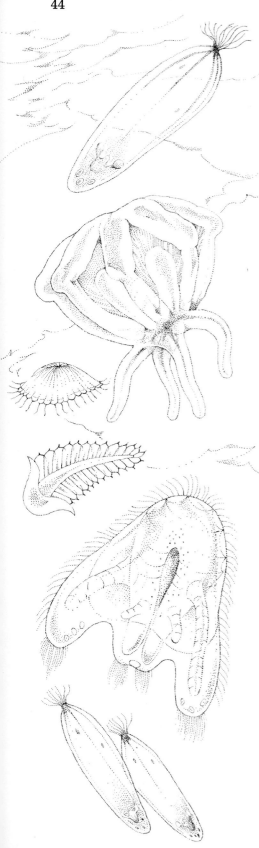

Soft bodies, no legs

Pretend that you are standing on a seashore. It is more than seven hundred million years ago. . . .

The early morning sunlight sparkles brightly on the water. Waves hiss as they roll up onto the shore. Beyond the shore, the land looks bare and empty for as far as you can see. Not a single plant grows, not a single animal moves. All the land, everywhere in the world, is just bare rock or sand, without any life.

But in the sea, there is a lot of life and movement. Tiny creatures with bodies soft as jelly swim or float in the water or crawl along on the sandy bottom. There are things that look like worms with feelers. There are animals that look like tiny cucumbers that you can see through. And there are other creatures that are bell-shaped blobs with many stubby "arms," or tentacles, that look like pieces of rope.

There are no fish, crabs, oysters, starfish, or other such animals in this long-ago sea. Such animals will not come into the world for a long, long time. But some of the tiny, soft, legless creatures that move about in the water are the beginnings of things to come. They are the ancestors of many kinds of animals with legs and shells that will come into the world much, much later.

Shells and many legs

On a muddy sea bottom, among piles of rock and clumps of feathery seaweed, a small animal creeps slowly along. From head to tail, it is about eight inches (20 centimeters) long. It looks a little like a thick, flat worm. But it has a thin shell, feelers, and many legs. Its legs have joints, like those of an insect. The edges of its shell form long points that curve down and drag in the mud. When the creature moves, it leaves a winding track in the mud. This little, many-legged animal is a trilobite (TRY luh byt).

As the trilobite scuttles along, its feelers jerk and wiggle. A bulgy eye, shaped like a half moon, stares out of each side of the shell that covers its head.

Rounding a clump of rocks, the trilobite finds itself among clusters of lumpy tubes that sit in the mud without moving. These tubes look like some kind of plant. But they are animals—animals called sponges. They never move. They live by digesting tiny plants and animals that simply drift into little openings in their bodies.

(continued on page 46)

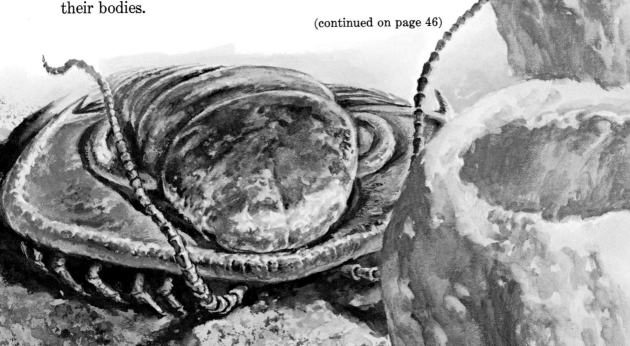

(continued from page 45)

The trilobite creeps among the sponges, its feelers twitching, searching for food. Suddenly, it stops and begins to dig in the mud. It soon uncovers a tiny, soft, dead worm.

As the trilobite eats, a cloud of tiny, round animals with legs like hairs drifts past it. These creatures are baby trilobites. They have just hatched out of eggs their mother buried in the mud. At another time, the grown-up trilobite might try to eat some of the tiny babies. But now it is busy with the worm.

Finishing its meal, the trilobite scuttles on. Near another cluster of sponges it comes upon a shell partly buried in the mud. It is a shell that another trilobite grew too big for—and climbed out of. Several times during its life a trilobite grows too big for its shell. Then the shell splits and the animal pushes its way out. For a while after this, its body is soft. Then, the outside of its body slowly hardens into a new shell.

As if tired of creeping, the trilobite springs upward

and begins to swim. It swims by wiggling the feathery little gills on each of its legs. It moves in quick little jerks that make it dodge from side to side. Soon, it disappears into the distance.

Trilobites were living in the sea six hundred million years ago, and probably long before that. Some were no bigger than a fingernail. Others were as much as a foot (30 centimeters) long. The word *trilobite* means "three parts." Scientists gave the animal this name because its body looks as if it were divided into three parts, lengthwise.

Trilobites were relatives of all the many-legged animals of today—crabs, lobsters, spiders, and insects. But there is nothing exactly like them in the world now. On the other hand, there are many kinds of sponges in the ocean today. They have changed very little since the time of the trilobites.

Trilobites and sponges were only two of the many kinds of animals living in the sea between six hundred million and five hundred million years ago. There were

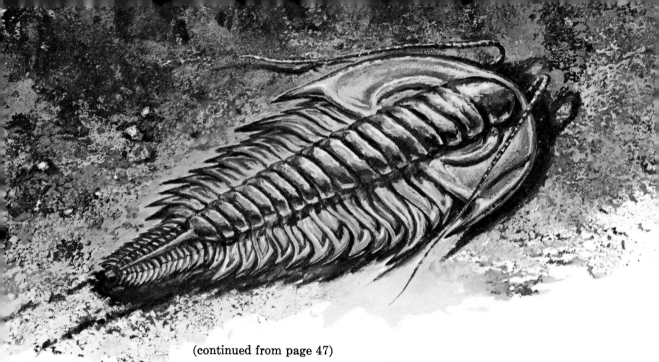

(continued from page 47)

lots of many-legged creatures, called trilobitomorphs
(try luh BYT uh mawrfs), scuttling about. And there
were jellyfish that looked much like glass umbrellas with
bunches of string hanging down from them.

Crawling over the rocks and through the mud were
creatures, called onychophorans (ahn uh KAHF uh ruhns),
that looked somewhat like caterpillars with stubby legs.
And there were tiny animals, somewhat like snails, with
curved, cone-shaped shells. They are called cephalopods
(SEHF uh luh pahdz), which means "head-foot." It is a
good name, because the lumpy foot they crawled on
was actually part of their head.

There were also enormous numbers of creatures
that looked much like clams. These creatures are
called brachiopods (BRAK ee uh pahdz), a name that
means "arm-foot." They had soft bodies covered with
two shells that were hinged together.

The world of that time was a world of mostly
small, many-legged or legless animals. Many of them
had shells. Some of these kinds of creatures still live
in the sea today. Others have been gone from the
world for hundreds of millions of years.

An animal like a trilobite

There's an animal living today that goes back to the time of the trilobites. Animals of its kind shared the seas with trilobites more than five hundred million years ago. It's a king crab, also called a horseshoe crab or horsefoot. But it isn't a true crab. It's a many-legged animal that's like a trilobite in some ways.

A king crab has twelve legs. Its body is covered by a round shell that looks like a horse's hoof. The shell of an average king crab is about nine inches (22 centimeters) wide. The king crab's round, bulgy eyes peer out of its shell, just as did the eyes of trilobites. A long, stiff tail, like a sharp spike, sticks out of the back of the shell.

King crabs live in fairly shallow water along seashores. They spend much of their time digging in the mud. They eat mostly worms or clams. Early in summer, female king crabs crawl up onto beaches to lay their eggs, which they bury in the mud or sand. When the babies hatch, they look even more like trilobites than the grown-ups do.

King crabs probably haven't changed their way of life much since the time of the trilobites. By studying these animals, we can see what life was like for many creatures five hundred million years ago.

Look Alikes
The king crab, or horseshoe crab (above), is a many-legged creature of today. But it looks much like a trilobite (below) of five hundred million years ago.

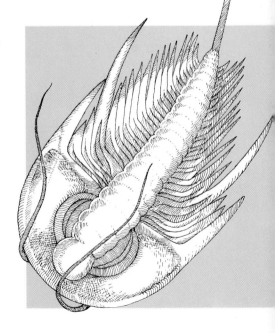

"Head-foots" and "flower" animals

A trilobite moved slowly over the sea bottom in search of food. It crept in and out among a bunch of what looked like brightly colored flowers growing on thick stems. This part of the sea bottom was like a garden. But the "flowers" were not flowers—they were animals! Animals that looked like flowers.

The trilobite came to a cluster of rocks. Suddenly, a number of long, snaky arms, or tentacles, reached out. The arms grabbed the trilobite. Helpless, the trilobite was pulled back into the mouth of a creature that lay hidden among the rocks.

The creature among the rocks was much like an octopus. It had a large, round head with two big,

staring eyes. Around its mouth were long, snaky
tentacles. Its head stuck out of a shell that looked
like a long, slim horn.

This was what it was like at the bottom of the sea
480 million years ago. Some new kinds of creatures
had now appeared in the world. There were clams and
starfish. There were creatures that looked more like
plants than animals. And there were creatures with
tentacles and shells.

The tentacled creatures were cephalopods, a name
that means "head-foot." The first cephalopods were
tiny creatures somewhat like snails. They were only a
few inches (centimeters) long, and crawled on a kind
of lumpy "foot." But during many millions of years,
the "foot" had become separate tentacles. And some
kinds of cephalopods had gotten much, much bigger.
One kind, with a long, pointed shell, was the biggest

(continued from page 51)
animal in the sea 480 million years ago. In fact, it was the largest animal that had ever lived in the world up to that time. From the tips of its stretched-out tentacles to the end of its shell, it was about thirteen feet (3.9 meters) long.

The creatures that looked like flowers on thick stems were crinoids (KRY noydz). *Crinoid* means "like a lily," and crinoids are often called "sea lilies." Millions of years ago, crinoids covered many parts of the sea bottom, but today only a few kinds are left. The parts of a crinoid that look like flower petals are its arms. With these arms a crinoid catches its food—tiny animals and plants that drift in the water.

Two other kinds of animals that looked like plants also lived in the sea 480 million years ago. Graptolites (GRAP tuh lyts) were tiny animals that lived in groups. The name means "painted stone." Each animal had a soft, cuplike shell, and the cups were joined together. Some groups looked like slim, long-stemmed plants drifting in the water. Other groups were like lacy branches or clusters of leaves. There are no graptolites now.

There was also coral in the sea by 480 million years ago. It was much like the coral that is in the sea today. Coral, too, is many tiny animals in little cups, all joined together. The clusters of cups look like lacy fans, deer antlers, or heads of lettuce.

The little coral animals, which are called polyps (PAHL ihps), are shaped like sacks with tentacles at one end. When all of the tentacles are sticking out of the cups, coral looks like a bunch of tiny flowers.

On the sea bottom, 480 million years ago, great clusters of brachiopods and clams lay on the sand and rocks. Sponges, corals, and crinoids were everywhere, like strange flowers in a great garden. Among them moved trilobites and other many-legged animals, as well as snails, starfish, and worms. Cephalopods lay in wait in hidden places. Jellyfish and floating graptolites drifted in the water.

The sea was filled with more life than ever. But scientists tell us that no animals of any kind yet lived on the land.

fossil graptolites

a fossil crinoid

Giant scorpions and jawless fish

A river winds down out of the mountains and flows to the sea. Where the river meets the sea, the water spreads out to form a lagoon, like a small lake. On the bottom of the lagoon, clams crawl about and dig themselves into the mud. Snails creep up and down the stems of underwater plants.

Among a thick bunch of plants, a small animal is swimming. Only about a foot (30 centimeters) long, it looks somewhat like a fish. But it is not much like any fish you have ever seen.

Its blunt, flat head is completely covered with thick bone. Tiny eyes on top of its head stare straight up out of the bone shell. Its body, which is shaped like an ice-cream cone, is covered with strips of bony armor. It has no fins, only a thick flap of skin on each side of its body, just behind the head. For a mouth, it has only a little round hole on the underside of its head.

This fishlike creature is called an ostracoderm (AHS truh koh durm), meaning "shell skin." It is very different from most of the other animals that live in this lagoon, or out in the sea. For it is one of the first kinds of animals to have a backbone.

The ostracoderm swims slowly, close to the muddy bottom. From time to time, it sinks down to push its mouth into the mud. This is how it eats—by sucking up tiny bits of dead plants and animals from the mud. Coming to the end of the thick cluster of plants, the ostracoderm moves out into the open.

Nearby, lying motionless in the mud, is a monster!

It is like a kind of giant insect, longer than a tall man.
A big, bulging eye stares out of each side of its round,
flat head. And, in the middle of its head, there are
two other tiny eyes set close together. A pair of long
legs, with crablike claws at the ends, are stretched out
in front of it. There are sharp "teeth" in the claws
that are used to crush any thin-shelled creature. But
the claws are not strong enough to crack through the

Look Alikes
The scorpion (above) that lives on land today looks very much like the eurypterid (below) of 415 million years ago.

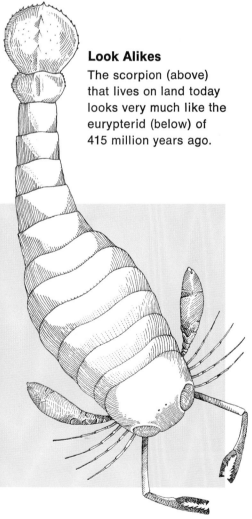

(continued from page 55)
bony armor of the ostracoderm. So the monster must wait for prey that it can crush and eat.

This animal lying quietly in the mud is a eurypterid (yu RIHP tuhr ihd), a name meaning "broad-winged." And two of the eurypterid's legs are shaped somewhat like broad, flat wings.

Eurypterids were many-legged animals, like insects, spiders, crabs, and lobsters. They looked very much like the scorpions that live on land now. There were several different kinds of eurypterids. Some of these prehistoric animals were only a few inches (centimeters) long, but others were as long as a man, or longer.

Ostracoderms and eurypterids lived about 415 million years ago. They lived mainly in streams, lakes, lagoons, and perhaps in shallow water along the edge of the sea. At the time they lived, there were still a great many trilobites, brachiopods, cephalopods, crinoids, and graptolites out in the sea.

Much of the land was still just bare rock, but along the banks of streams and on the shores of bays and lagoons there was a bit of greenery. Some kinds of water plants had slowly moved up out of the water and were able to live in air. Life was beginning to conquer the land.

The Age of Fishes

A forest of strange, snaky-looking plants stretches away for some distance on each side of a river. But beyond the forest, the land is bare and empty. The river, however, is full of living things. Along the river bottom, many kinds of ostracoderms, covered with bony armor, browse in the mud. Eurypterids of all sizes lie hidden among water plants, or swim swiftly in search of prey. Snails creep slowly about in the mud or crawl up the stems of plants.

A school of small, scaly fish comes gliding swiftly through the water. They are little fish, only a few inches (centimeters) long. Many pairs of sharp points, like little thorns, run along the underside of their bodies. The two fins on their backs also end in tough,

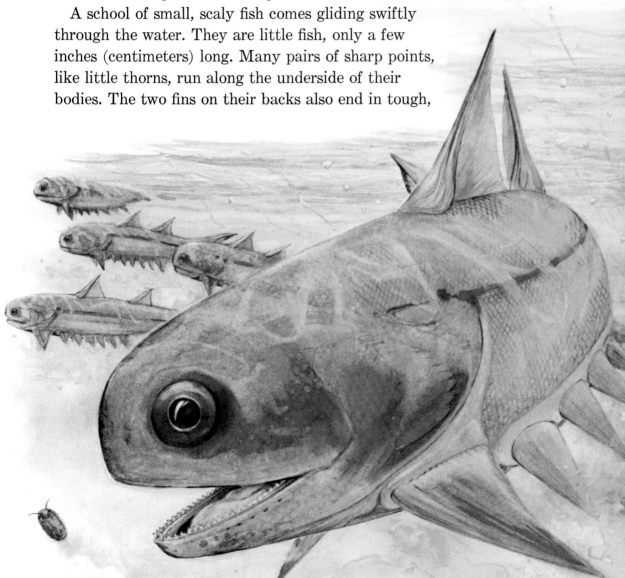

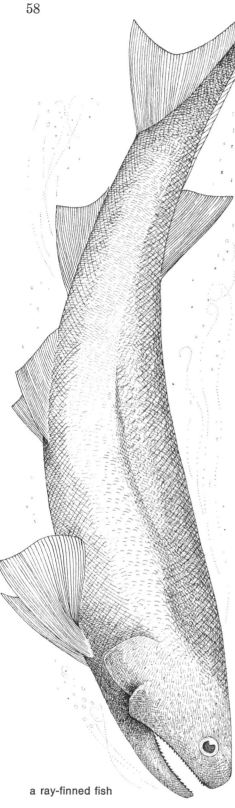

a ray-finned fish

(continued from page 57)

sharp points. Tiny, diamond-shaped scales cover their bodies.

A small, many-legged creature suddenly comes skittering through the water in front of the school of fish. With a quick flick of its tail, one fish at the front of the school darts forward. Its mouth opens wide, showing rows of tiny, sharp teeth. In an instant, the many-legged creature is caught and swallowed.

These little fish lived about four hundred million years ago. They are the first animals we know of that had jaws. Because of the thornlike points on their bellies and fins, these little fish are called acanthodians (ak uhn THOH dee uhnz), which means "thornlike."

Jaws were an important new thing in the world. They were a big help to such creatures as fish. Fish have no arms with which to grab things. As long as creatures like the ostracoderms had only holes for mouths, they could eat only food that didn't move much. But jaws are really a trap for catching food. Fish with jaws could eat anything they could catch and swallow. This meant there was a lot more food for them. They were able to increase and spread out in the world.

So, by about 350 million years ago, many kinds of fish with jaws were living in lakes, rivers, and the sea. Some, called ray-fins—little creatures about nine inches (22 centimeters) long—were the ancestors of the kinds of fish that live in the world now. The first sharks were also living then. They were slim, streamlined animals from about two to five feet (60 to 150 centimeters) long.

One kind of fish was able to put its head out of water and breathe air for a short time. It was a small fish, only about ten inches (25 centimeters) long, but it was to be a very important animal. On its underside were four short, thick fins, almost like clumsy legs. Scientists think these fish, called fringe-fins, were the ancestors of all the four-footed animals that now live on the land!

There were giant fish at that time, too. One of these fish was about thirty feet (9 meters) long, with a huge head and sharp, jagged jaws, like those of a snapping turtle. Its head was covered with pieces of thick, bony armor. It must have been the terror of the seas!

The period of time from 405 million to 345 million years ago, when these many kinds of fish appeared, is called the Age of Fishes. It might be said that fish were the kings of the world during that time. But the water was filled with many other kinds of animals, too.

There were still a great many trilobites. Some of them had become quite strange in appearance, with knobs and long, sharp horns on their shells. Some had become

a fringe-finned fish

(continued from page 59)

quite large. One kind was a giant, more than two feet (60 centimeters) long.

There were still many kinds of brachiopods, corals, and sponges. Crinoids and starfish were increasing in number, and there were also more clams, oysters, and snails than before. But graptolites were nearly all gone. So were the cephalopods with the long, pointed shells—their place was being taken by cephalopods with curled-up shells.

In the many lakes and rivers, eurypterids were still plentiful and there were also a few other kinds of many-legged creatures. But by the end of the Age of Fishes, most of the little bone-armored ostracoderms were gone.

It was during the Age of Fishes that a very great thing happened. Some kinds of animals left the water and began to live on the land.

giant armored fish

shark

A leftover fish from the Age of Fishes

One kind of fish that first appeared during the Age of Fishes is called a coelacanth (SEE luh kanth). The name means "hollow spine."

Coelacanths lived in the ocean for many millions of years. Scientists thought they had died out by about seventy million years ago. But, from fossil skeletons of coelacanths, scientists worked out how these fish must have looked and lived.

Then, in 1938, a wonderful thing happened. Some fishermen caught a strange-looking fish off the coast of South Africa. They had never seen anything like it. When their ship docked, they took the fish to a museum. The museum director got in touch with a famous scientist who came to look at the fish. He was amazed to see that it was a coelacanth!

Catching the coelacanth had been a lucky accident. Scientists now know that these fish live in deep water and seldom come up far enough to be caught. But once scientists knew these fish still existed, they were able to catch others for study.

The coelacanths are much like their prehistoric ancestors of many millions of years ago, except they are bigger—three to five feet (90 to 150 centimeters) long. Their bodies are bluish-gray and covered with big scales. They eat small fish.

Scientists were delighted to see that most of what they had worked out about how coelacanths looked and lived was right. It was proof that many of their other ideas about prehistoric animals were probably right, too.

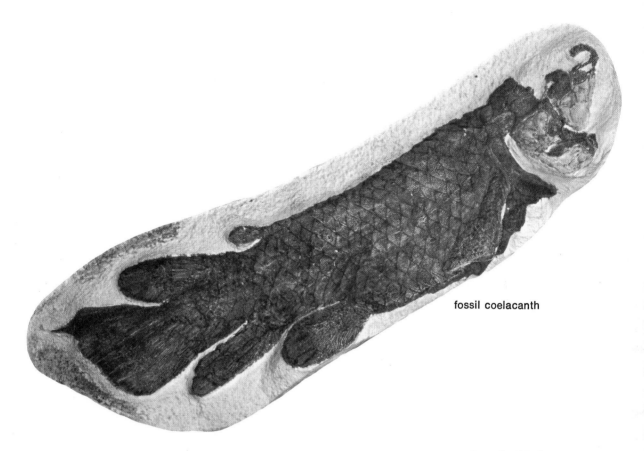

fossil coelacanth

coelacanth of today

How big were they?

Compared to a child, some prehistoric water creatures were huge. Others were quite small. Most trilobites were even smaller than the one shown here. But some were much bigger.

eurypterid
9 feet (2.7 meters) long

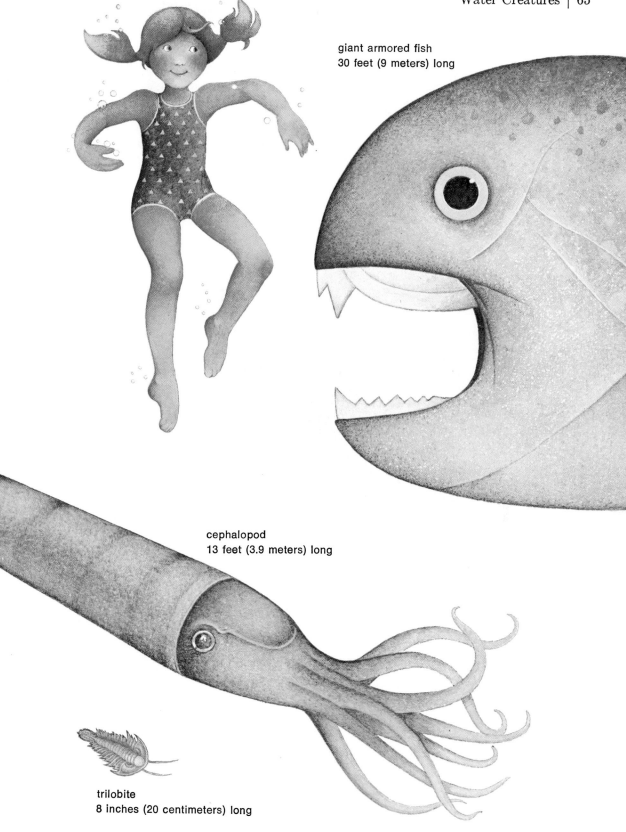

giant armored fish
30 feet (9 meters) long

cephalopod
13 feet (3.9 meters) long

trilobite
8 inches (20 centimeters) long

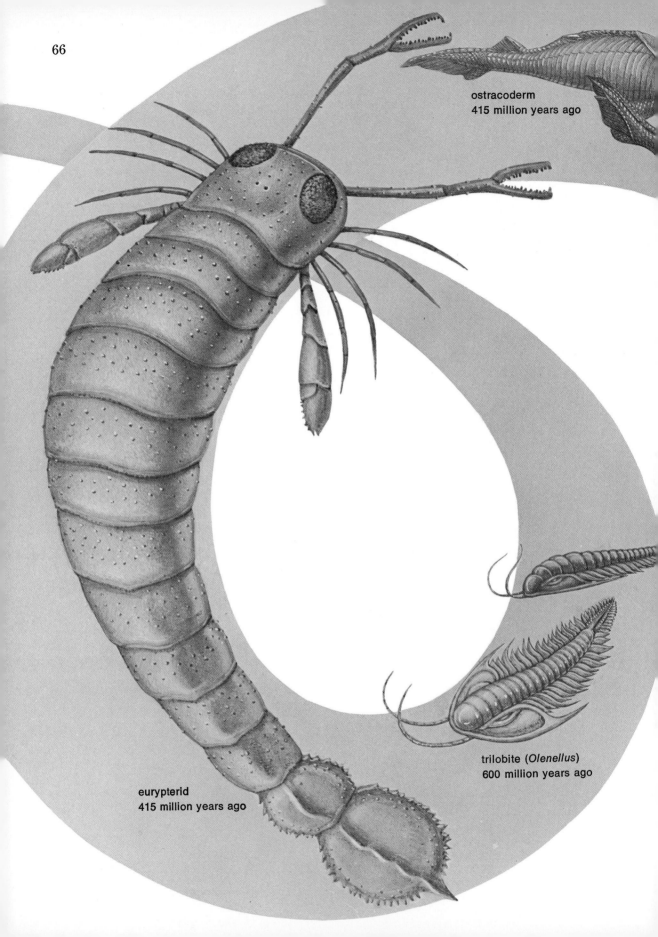

ostracoderm
415 million years ago

trilobite (*Olenellus*)
600 million years ago

eurypterid
415 million years ago

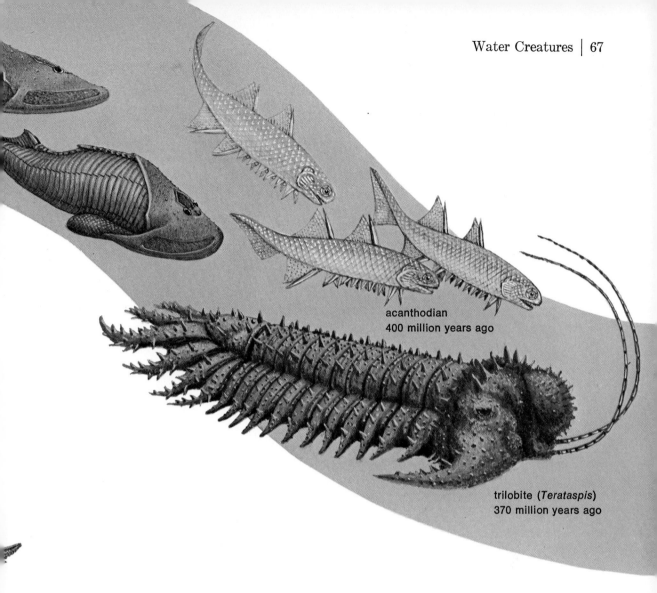

acanthodian
400 million years ago

trilobite (*Terataspis*)
370 million years ago

When did they live?

The animals shown here are all water creatures that lived between 600 million and about 370 million years ago. During all that time there were trilobites, ranging in size from little *Olenellus* to the "giant" *Terataspis*. Eurypterids and other many-legged creatures were common. Some of them became the first land animals. Ostracoderms were one of the first animals to have a backbone, and acanthodians were the first to have jaws.

Life Moves
to the Land

Scientists think that the land was bare and lifeless until about 450 million years ago. Then, a little at a time, during many millions of years, living things moved from the water onto the land.

Probably the first living things to come out of the water onto land were the kinds of plants called algae (AL jee). Slowly, very slowly, some of the algae that lived near the shore became able to live in air. During countless years, these plants spread up out of the water onto the beaches.

As time went by, the plants spread ever farther onto the land. As plants died, their remains became mixed with crumbled rock and water. In time, this mixture became the first soil.

As millions of years went by, the plants changed. They became true land plants. They grew in soil that was made by earlier plants. The land, gray and bare for billions of years, grew green.

And, after the plants, animals began to move out of the water onto the land.

on the next page ▶
Between 450 million and 350 million years ago, plants, many-legged creatures, and fish such as *Eusthenopteron* became able to live on land.

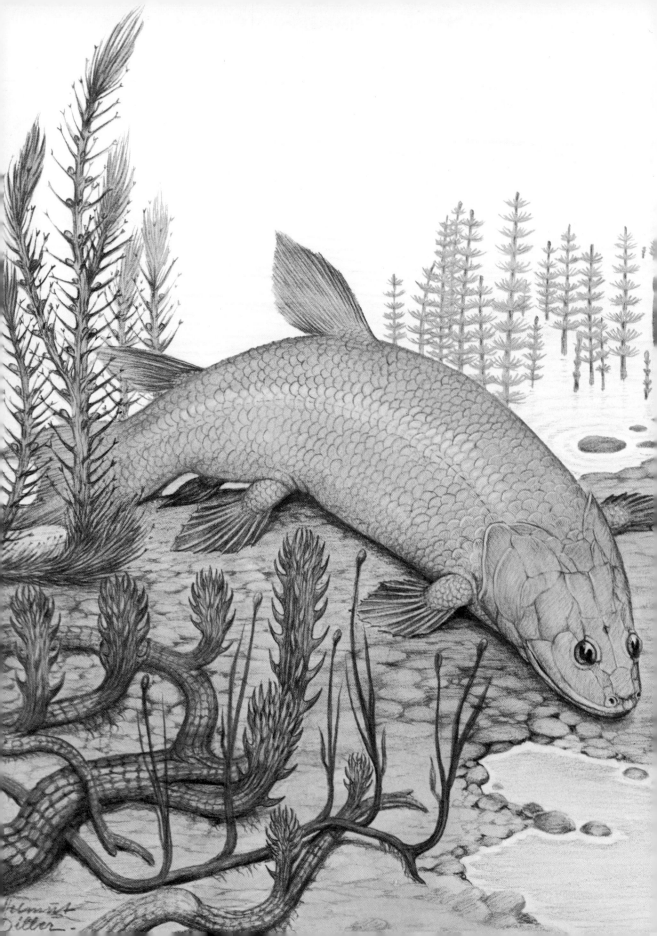

Helmut
Diller -

A scorpion called *Palaeophonus* (pay lee uh FOHN uhs) was probably the first animal to leave the water and live on land.

Many legs on the land

It isn't easy to imagine the land as it was about 420 million years ago. It was very different from the way it is now.

There were no trees. There was no grass. But there were strange-looking plants that grew along the edges of rivers, lakes, and bays. These plants had long, snaky stems that curled over the ground. Little roots from the stems went into the soil. Thick stalks, covered with leaves that looked like little green fish scales, grew up from some of the stems. Other plants had thin stalks with knobs on the ends. Some plants were like clusters of wide, green ribbons.

Among all these strange-looking plants moved the first animals that lived on land. Scientists think that the first animals to leave the water and become land dwellers were scorpions, related to the eurypterids. Soon after, other animals came out of the water, too—creatures that were somewhat like centipedes and spiders.

For a long time, such creatures might have lived in shallow water, moving back and forth between the water and the land. After millions of years they became true land animals, that could breathe in air. For millions of years, the land belonged to these many-legged creatures.

The crawling fish

The sun beats down on a strange forest. The trunks and branches of the trees are covered with stiff little leaves, like scaly skin. There has been no rain now for some time, and all the leaves are yellow. The ground is baked hard.

A pond in the forest is almost dry. The little water left in it looks like thick soup. Suddenly, a wet, scaly head pokes up out of the water. Two round eyes stare about.

Slowly, the creature climbs out of the pond. It is a fish. Moving on its four lower fins, which are like thick tassels, it crawls off into the forest!

Such a scene might well have taken place about 370 million years ago. Scientists think that certain kinds of fish that lived in shallow ponds became able to live on land for short periods of time. They could also crawl on their thick fins. So, if a pond began to dry up, or to run short of food, the fish left. They crawled up onto land and looked for another pond with cleaner, deeper water and more food.

Some kinds of fish are able to do this today. But the crawling fish of long ago were something brand new in the world. Some of them were the ancestors of the first four-footed animals.

Act Alikes
The mudskipper (above) is a fish of today that can walk on land. *Eusthenopteron* (yoos thehn AHP tuhr ahn), a prehistoric fish (below), could also walk on land.

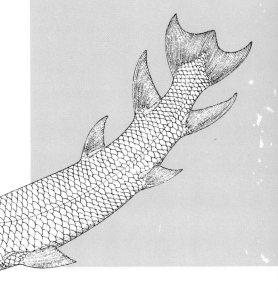

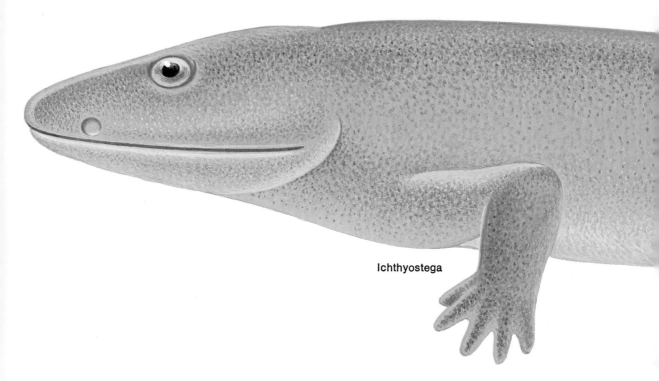

Ichthyostega

The first four-footed animals

For millions of years, fish with four thick fins on their undersides often left their ponds and crawled about on land. And slowly they changed. Although they spent most of their time in water, they became able to breathe in air. In time, their four thick fins became short, clumsy legs. They were the world's first four-footed animals.

These new creatures looked very much like fish, but they had legs instead of fins. They laid their eggs in water, as fish do. The babies that came from the eggs stayed in the water until they grew up. Then they

became able to breathe in air and go onto the land.
These creatures were the first of the group of animals
we call amphibians—animals that are mostly born in
water and spend most of their time in water, but can
also live on land. Frogs, toads, salamanders, and the
strange, wormlike animals called caecilians (see SIHL
ee uhns) are the amphibians of today.

The oldest amphibian we know of lived about 350
million years ago. It has been named *Ichthyostega*
(ihk thee uh STAY guh), which means "fish-skull roof."
It was given this name because the top of its skull
is the same as that of the fish that was its ancestor.
Ichthyostega was about three feet (1 meter) long.

The swampy forest

A vast, swampy forest simmers in the hot afternoon sunshine. As far as an eye might see, there is a thick jumble of trees. Some of the trees have smooth, soft trunks with bunches of sword-shaped leaves at the very top. Others have very short, curved branches that grow in many rings around the trunk. And still other trees have trunks that look as if they are covered with scales shaped like diamonds.

The muddy ground in which these trees grow is covered with a thick tangle of ferns. There are rotting stumps and trunks of fallen trees everywhere. Great clumps of stringy moss cover many of them. Snaky vines with feathery leaves twine about them.

The forest is very quiet. No bird calls sound among the trees. There are no birds anywhere in the world. No squirrels or monkeys dart and chatter in the trees. There are no furry animals of any kind, yet. But there are insects—the world's first flying creatures—as well as other many-legged animals. And there are great numbers of amphibians. This is a vast, swampy forest of three hundred million years ago.

Great ponds and pools lie everywhere among the trees. The air above the ponds and pools is the hunting ground of giant dragonflies. Their great, shimmering wings spread out as long as a man's arms. Small insects that buzz too near these creatures are seized and eaten. These dragonflies, named *Meganeura* (mehg uh NUR uh), are the largest winged insects that have ever lived.

The ponds and pools, shining in the sunlight, seem calm and lifeless. But scores of creatures swim, hunt, and eat in them.

A slim creature, about two feet (60 centimeters)

(continued from page 77)
long, wriggles swiftly across the top of the water in one of the ponds. It looks like a snake, but there are no snakes yet. This animal is a legless amphibian called *Ophiderpeton* (oh fih DUHR peh tahn).

Suddenly, a large shape shoots out from behind a great tree trunk that lies half buried in the water. It is a creature with a large head, a long body and tail, and tiny legs. This giant is *Eogyrinus* (ee oh jy RIHN uhs), an amphibian fifteen feet (4.5 meters) long. In an instant, it swallows up the small, snakelike amphibian.

Many other kinds of amphibians, as well as fish and eurypterids live in the pond. There are also dragonfly babies, which are born in water, and many kinds of water insects. On the pond's muddy bottom, snails crawl and worms burrow.

For all these creatures, life is an endless struggle to find food and to stay alive. They spend much of their

(continued from page 79)

time swimming in search of prey or lying in wait for something to pass near enough to be seized. Bigger creatures prey upon smaller ones. But many of the smaller creatures often eat the babies of bigger ones.

The floor of the forest is also the home or hunting place of many animals. Scorpions and spiders scuttle about among the ferns. Giant cockroaches, four inches (10 centimeters) long, swarm among the rotting logs. Three-foot (1-meter) long *Diplovertebron*s (dihp luh

VUHR tuh brahns) and other small amphibians creep through the mud and plants after these insects.

There are also a few kinds of another sort of animal in this forest of three hundred million years ago. These animals look much like small amphibians. But they are a little quicker moving and, perhaps, just a little smarter. They are not born in water, like amphibians. They are a new kind of animal, descended from some of the amphibians. They are the first of the group of animals we call reptiles.

How big were they?

Many amphibians of 350 million to 300 million years ago were rather small, like *Ichthyostega*. But *Eogyrinus* was a giant. *Meganeura*, a dragonfly, had a wingspread nearly as wide as a child's outspread arms.

Eogyrinus
15 feet (4.5 meters) long

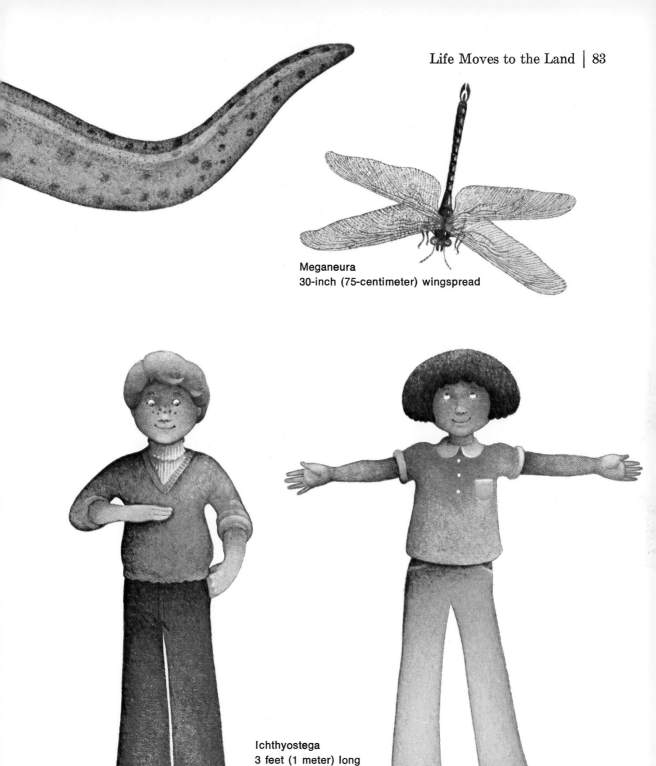

Meganeura
30-inch (75-centimeter) wingspread

Ichthyostega
3 feet (1 meter) long

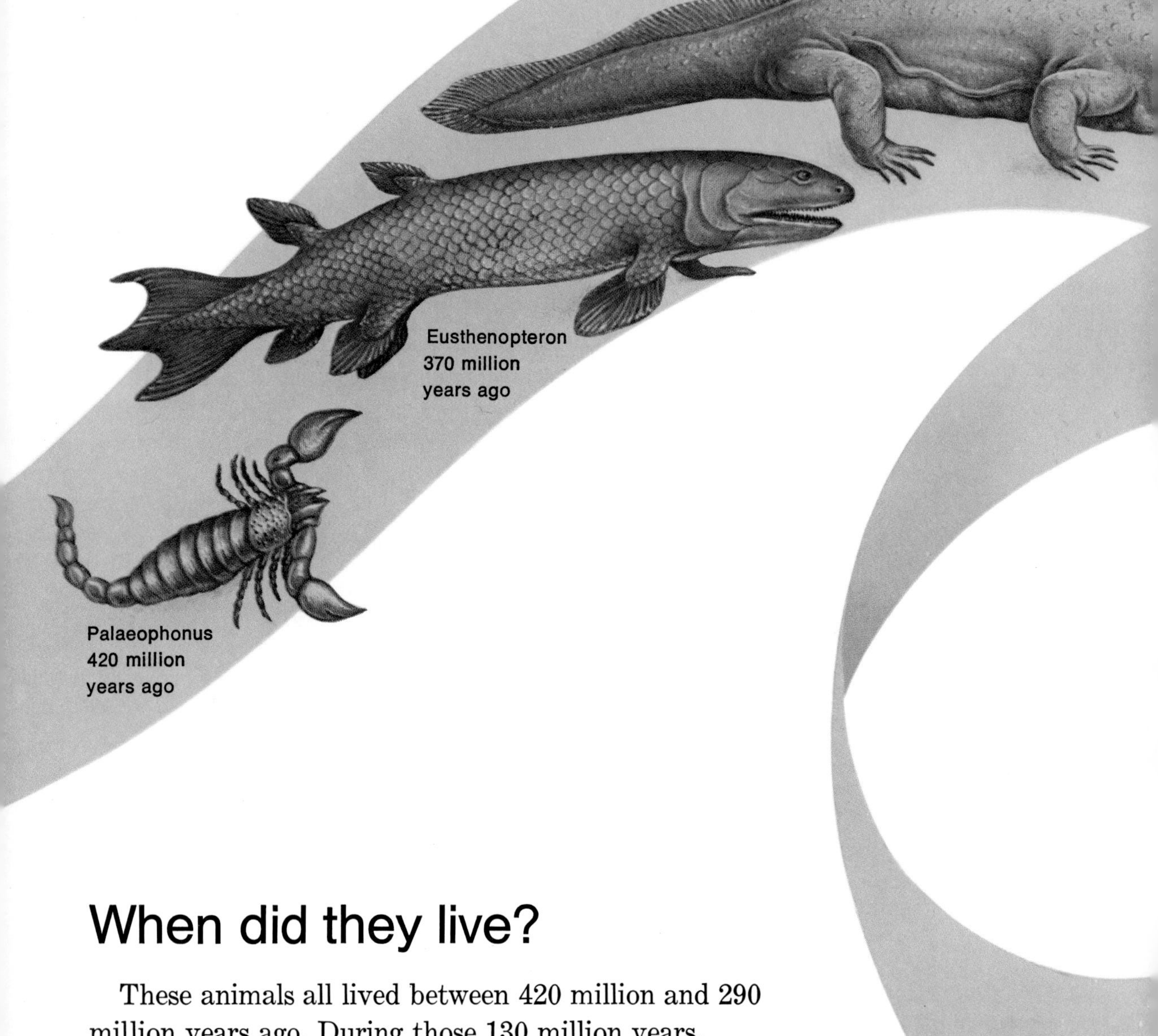

Eusthenopteron
370 million
years ago

Palaeophonus
420 million
years ago

When did they live?

These animals all lived between 420 million and 290
million years ago. During those 130 million years,
many important things happened. Scorpions, such as
Palaeophonus, left the water and became the first land
animals. Fish, such as *Eusthenopteron*, gave rise to the
first four-footed land animals, such as *Ichthyostega*.
And insects were the first to develop wings. For
millions of years, insects, other many-legged creatures,
and amphibians, such as *Diplovertebron*, were the only
kinds of land animals.

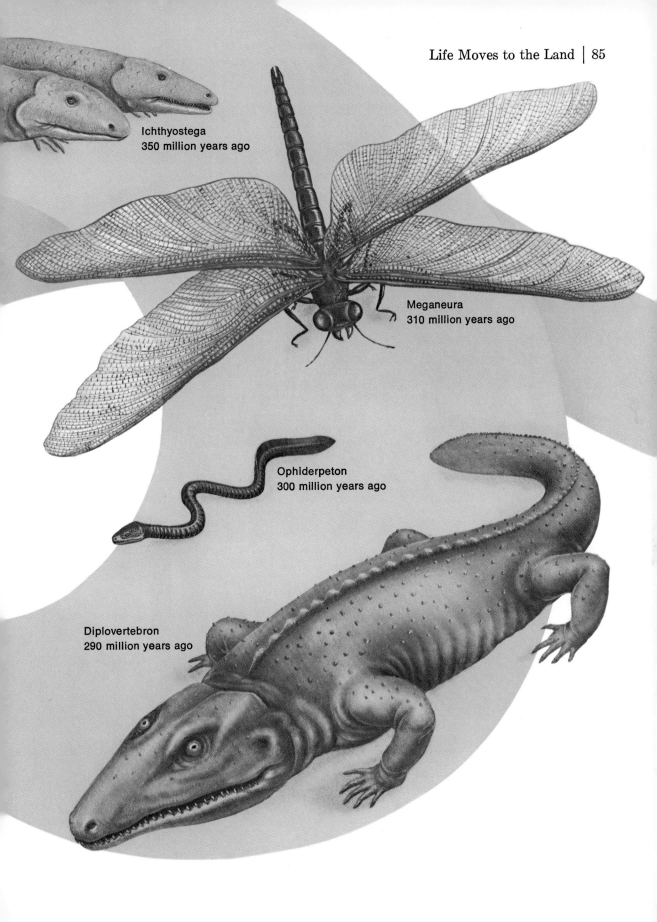

Ichthyostega
350 million years ago

Meganeura
310 million years ago

Ophiderpeton
300 million years ago

Diplovertebron
290 million years ago

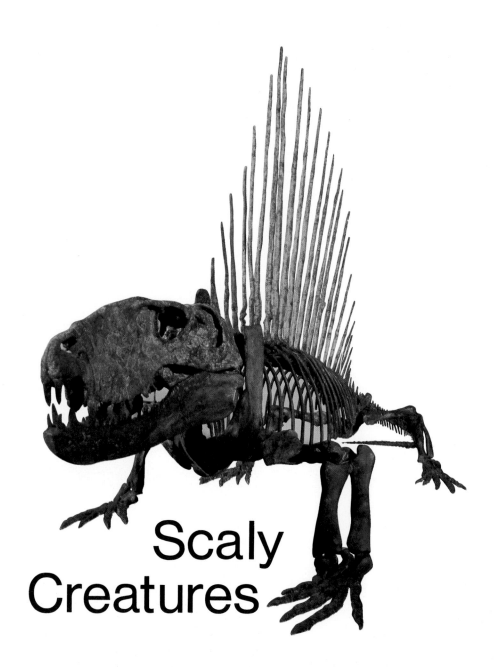

Scaly
Creatures

The amphibians of long ago had to stay near water, just as frogs, toads, and other amphibians must do today. They had to lay their soft, jellylike eggs in water or the sun would dry them up. The babies that came from the eggs could only breathe in water. They had to stay in water until they grew up and were able to breathe air.

But scientists think that about 310 million years ago, some amphibians began to change. They became more and more able to stay on land. After a time, some of them began to lay a new kind of egg—an egg that was covered by a shell. Such eggs did not have to be laid in water. And the babies that hatched from these eggs were able to breathe air and live on the land.

These new creatures were the animals that we now call reptiles—scaly skinned, cold-blooded animals that lay their eggs on land. They were the ancestors of lizards, snakes, crocodiles, and the other reptiles of today. In time, they would become the rulers of the world—a rule that would last for 210 million years.

on the next page ▶
By about three hundred million years ago, early reptiles such as *Hylonomus* were living on land and laying eggs with shells.

A fossil of *Romeriscus,*
the oldest reptile known.

The coming of the reptiles

A yellow moon glowed brightly above a great, dark forest. Winged insects hummed through the air and giant cockroaches scuttled among the ferns and fallen tree trunks. In the darkness among the trees, and in the black water of swamps, many different kinds of four-legged creatures were moving about.

Most of these four-legged animals were amphibians. An amphibian is an animal that lays its eggs in water and spends its life in or near water. But some of these amphibians were beginning to take on a new way of life. They were changing into something else.

These changing amphibians laid their eggs in water, as other amphibians did. But they spent most of their time on land. They were slowly becoming land animals instead of water animals. As millions of years passed, they changed in other ways. They became a little smarter and a bit quicker than amphibians. And they began to lay eggs that were protected by shells—eggs that could be laid on land. These new animals were no longer amphibians. They had become reptiles.

What did the first reptiles look like? They were probably very much like the amphibians they came from, but their skin may have been more scaly. The first reptile we know of lived about three hundred million years ago. Less than two feet (60 centimeters) long, it is named *Romeriscus* (roh muhr IHS kuhs), after a famous scientist, Alfred Romer.

As time went on, the number of reptiles increased. Some of them began to move out of the big, swampy forests. Slowly, the reptiles took over the world.

The new world of the reptiles

By 280 million years ago, many parts of the earth had changed. The climate had become cooler and drier. Many of the great swamps had dried up. The forests of soft trees had been replaced by the first kinds of evergreen trees. Chains of rugged mountains had pushed up in parts of the land. There were many deserts. And in the far southern parts of the world, sheets of ice and snow covered much of the land.

The warmest parts of the world were filled with animals. There were still no furry animals or any birds, but there were many new kinds of insects. Some of these were like insects of today, such as stone flies and lacewings.

The lakes and rivers were the homes of many kinds of amphibians and a few reptiles that had taken to the water. There were many kinds of fish, and a few sharks. Many-legged creatures were numerous, but the eurypterids that had once ruled the water were now nearly all gone.

The seas swarmed with fish. The sea bottoms were "forests" of corals and crinoids. Brachiopods were still plentiful, but there were only about four kinds of trilobites left. And there were a great many of the cephalopods with coiled shells.

The land belonged to the reptiles. Some of these reptiles were small, fast-moving insect-eaters. Some were large plant-eaters. And some were sharp-toothed hunters that ate other reptiles and amphibians. But none of these reptiles were like the reptiles of today. There were no snakes, lizards, turtles, or alligators.

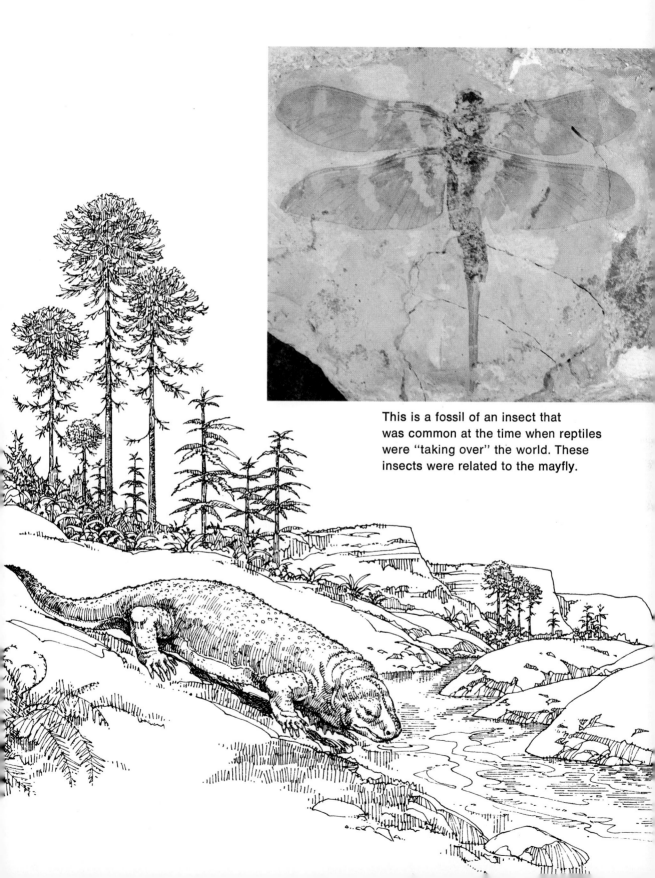

This is a fossil of an insect that was common at the time when reptiles were "taking over" the world. These insects were related to the mayfly.

Water reptiles

Sunlight sparkled on the water. Fish darted and drifted in the silvery brightness. Many-legged creatures swam about or crept upon the bottom.

A small four-legged animal, no more than two feet (60 centimeters) long, moved swiftly through the water. It had scaly skin, a long, flat tail, and webbed feet. Its long, thin jaws bristled with tiny, needlelike teeth. The creature swam as easily as a fish, its legs tucked against its body and its long tail wiggling from side to side.

This scaly animal was a reptile called *Mesosaurus* (mehs uh SAWR uhs) that lived about 275 million years ago. Mesosaurus was one of the first kinds of water reptiles. Some scientists think these little animals lived in lakes or rivers, others think they lived in the sea. They probably ate tiny many-legged creatures that they strained through their teeth, like some whales do, now.

Reptiles are true land animals. They are born on the land and only breathe in air. But even so, the first reptiles probably spent much of their time in the water, just as the amphibians did. After a time, most reptiles moved onto the land and stayed there. But some kinds of reptiles stayed in the water. And other kinds of reptiles left the land after a while and went back to the water.

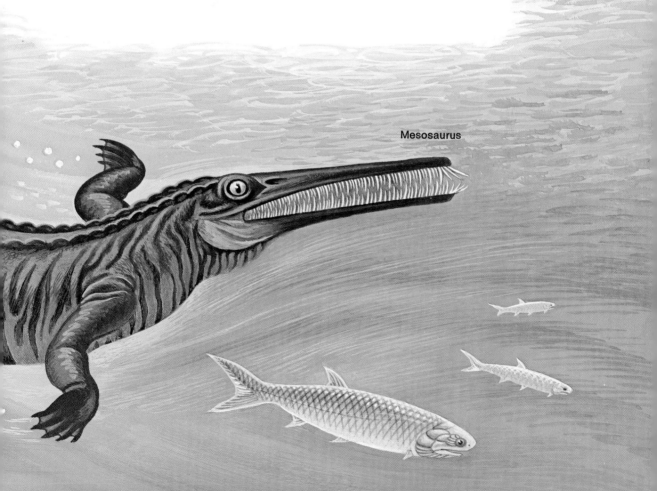

Mesosaurus

The fossil skeleton of a *Dimetrodon*.

Reptiles with "sails"

About 270 million years ago, in what is now the state of Texas, there were two very strange reptiles. They were not quite like any other reptile that ever lived, then or now. Each of these animals had a huge fin, much like a big sail, growing up out of its back. No other reptile of that time had such a fin. And no reptile of today has one.

One of these reptiles is called *Dimetrodon* (dy MEH truh dahn), a name that means "two sizes of teeth." *Dimetrodon* was a sharp-toothed flesh-eater about ten feet (3 meters) long.

The other reptile, called *Edaphosaurus* (ee daf uh SAWR uhs), or "earth lizard," was a plant-eater. It was somewhat smaller than *Dimetrodon*, and may sometimes have been a *Dimetrodon*'s dinner.

What could the animals' big fin have been for? Well, most scientists think the fins probably worked as a sort of air conditioning and heating machine!

Reptiles are cold-blooded animals. This means that their body temperature changes with the temperature of the air. In the early morning, after the coolness of night, a reptile's body is often cold. When its body is cold, a reptile cannot move quickly. The animal then has to lie in the sun until its blood warms up. And when a reptile's blood gets too warm during the day, the reptile must lie in the shade until it cools off. Otherwise, it will die.

If the fin helped *Dimetrodon* and *Edaphosaurus* warm up or cool off quickly, they wouldn't have had to lie in the sun or the shade for very long. Then they would have had more time to look for food.

Dimetrodon

On the great plain

Some reptiles were drinking from a stream. The reptiles looked clumsy. They had bulky bodies, thick legs, and stubby tails. Their heads looked for all the world like that of a baby cow, or calf. Because of this, these animals are called *Moschops* (MAH skahps), a name that means "calf-face." Their teeth stuck out in a way that made them seem to be foolishly smiling. The biggest of these animals were about seven feet (2.1 meters) long and five feet (1.5 meters) high.

Finishing their drink, several of the "calf-faces" waddled over to a clump of stubby plants. There the creatures began to eat, neatly snipping off leaves with their stuck-out teeth.

Over the top of a nearby rise in the ground another animal appeared. Slowly, it made its way down to the stream. It, too, was a bulky, clumsy-looking reptile. But it was bigger than the other animals, and the back of its neck was covered with hard, bony spikes. A pair of spiky horns stuck out of its cheeks. It was a *Bradysaurus* (bra dee SAWR uhs), a name that means "slow lizard."

The plant-eating "calf-faces" paid no attention to this newcomer. Like them, the *Bradysaurus* was a plant-eater. It offered no danger. They continued to munch leaves.

(continued on page 100)

(continued from page 98)

But there was danger only a short distance away! Behind another low rise in the ground, a very different kind of creature was prowling. About the size of a big dog, it was slim and quick moving, with slender legs. A pair of long, sharp teeth, like curved daggers, stuck out of its mouth. Although it was a reptile, it looked somewhat like a dog or a wolf. For this reason it is called *Lycaenops* (LY kayn ahps), or "wolf-face."

The *Lycaenops* climbed to the top of the rise. At the sight of the animals near the stream it stopped short. Then it rushed toward them.

At once the big clumsy plant-eaters scattered, running for their lives. But the wolflike hunter had picked its prey. Catching up to one of the smallest plant-eaters, it stabbed its daggerlike teeth savagely into the animal's neck. As the other plant-eaters disappeared, the *Lycaenops* began to feed on its kill.

All of this might have happened about 230 million years ago. At that time, these reptiles lived on a great plain that stretched across part of what is now South Africa. Very similar kinds of reptiles lived in many other parts of the world.

Hairy reptiles?

It would be a strange sight indeed to see a snake, or a lizard, or an alligator that had hair instead of scales! All the reptiles today have scaly skin. But scientists think that at one time there *were* reptiles with hair instead of scales!

Some of the reptiles that lived about 220 million years ago were different from other reptiles. They were shaped more like dogs or wolves than like lizards or crocodiles. Their teeth and bones were different from the teeth and bones of most reptiles. They were probably warm-blooded instead of cold-blooded as are reptiles. And, although they may have had scaly skin, it's much more likely that they had hair.

Just as some amphibians had once changed into reptiles, these reptiles were changing, too. Some were on the path to becoming a new kind of animal—the kind of animal that is called a mammal. Mammals are hairy, warm-blooded animals that feed their babies milk. Dogs and cats, cows and horses, dolphins and whales—and humans—are all mammals.

After millions of years, the descendants of one kind of hairy reptile became the first kind of mammal.

The reptile called *Cynognathus* (sihn uh NATH uhs), or "dog-jaw," may have been scaly, as most reptiles are. But it may have been hairy, as mammals are.

The first two-legged animals

For hundreds of millions of years, all the animals that lived on land were either many-legged creatures, such as insects, or four-legged amphibians and reptiles. But about 220 million years ago, one kind of reptile became able to walk and run on its back legs. It was the first animal in the world to move on two legs.

These reptiles were little creatures, less than three feet (1 meter) long. They ran swiftly on their back legs, with their long, slender tails stretched straight out for balance. They probably held their front legs

a thecodont

up in front of their chests, the way a kangaroo holds its paws when it hops.

These little animals belonged to a group of reptiles thecodonts (THEE kuh dahnts). The name means "teeth in sockets." Quick-moving, skillful hunters, they ate insects and smaller reptiles. They were soon more and more numerous. By 150 million years ago, their descendants had moved into all parts of the world. And some of their descendants were giants. For these little reptiles that ran on two legs were the ancestors of—the dinosaurs!

Lycaenops
4 feet (1.2 meters) long

How big were they?

None of the reptiles that lived between three hundred million and two hundred million years ago were very big. You could have peeked over *Edaphosaurus*'s big fin, and *Lycaenops* was no bigger than a large dog.

thecodont
3 feet (1 meter) long

Edaphosaurus
10 feet (3 meters) long

Hylonomus
300 million years ago

Edaphosaurus
270 million
years ago

Moschops
230 million years ago

When did they live?

The animals shown here are all reptiles that lived between 300 million and 210 million years ago. Early reptiles, such as *Hylonomus*, were small. Later, many reptiles, such as *Edaphosaurus, Bradysaurus,* and *Moschops,* were large, active creatures. Reptiles such as *Cynognathus* began to develop into warm-blooded, hairy animals. Some of the reptiles called thecodonts were the ancestors of the dinosaurs and of birds.

thecodont
210 million years ago

Cynognathus
220 million years ago

Bradysaurus
230 million years ago

The Age of Reptiles

For about 165 million years, reptiles were the rulers of the world. They were the largest and most dangerous animals on the land and in the sea. Some even became masters of the air—reptiles with wings. This period—from about 230 million to 65 million years ago—when reptiles ruled the earth, is called the Age of Reptiles.

At the beginning of the Age of Reptiles the earth's climate was rather cool and dry. For a time, great sheets of ice and snow covered some southern parts of the world. Then, slowly, the climate changed. Much of the world became warm and moist all year long. Great swamps, upland plains, and vast forests of palm trees and evergreen trees appeared.

It was during the Age of Reptiles that the first birds appeared. So did the first mammals—tiny, furry beasts that looked somewhat like mice. And it was during the Age of Reptiles that there lived some of the largest and most awesome creatures that ever walked on land—the reptiles called dinosaurs.

on the next page ▶
By 190 million years ago, large reptiles, such as the dinosaurs *Plateosaurus* (left) and *Ornithosuchus* (right), ruled the earth.

The discovery of dinosaurs

Today, nearly everyone knows what a dinosaur was. But, until about 150 years ago no one even suspected that such creatures had ever existed!

The story of the discovery of the dinosaurs began in England. It was a pleasant March morning in 1822. Dr. Gideon Mantell was visiting one of his patients, who lived out in the country. Dr. Mantell's wife was with him. It was such a nice day that she decided to go for a walk while the doctor saw his patient.

As Mrs. Mantell walked, she came to a pile of rocks by the roadside. The rocks had been dumped there by workmen repairing the road. Something in the pile caught Mrs. Mantell's eye. She bent down to look at it more closely.

Half buried in one piece of rock was what looked like a huge tooth. She was almost certain it was a fossil. Mrs. Mantell knew what fossils were. Her husband collected and studied fossils as a hobby. She was sure he would want to see this big fossil tooth, so she picked up the piece of rock.

Dr. Mantell was indeed delighted. He had never seen anything like this tooth. For the next few weeks, whenever he could, he went back to where his wife had found it, hoping to discover others. Sure enough, he found several more teeth. He also found several bones that must have come from the same animal.

But what kind of animal could have had such teeth? Mantell badly wanted to know. He sent the teeth and bones to a famous French scientist, Baron Georges Cuvier. Baron Cuvier examined them and sent word that the teeth came from an ancient rhinoceros. The bones, he said, were those of an ancient hippopotamus.

(continued on page 116)

(continued from page 114)

Mantell didn't think that was right. He was sure that the teeth and bones were much too old to have come from a rhinoceros or hippopotamus. He continued to study them, comparing them to other fossils, trying to find what kind of creature they were from.

Finally, in 1825, he had a stroke of luck. One day, while studying at a museum, he met a man named Samuel Stutchbury. Mr. Stutchbury was an expert on the lizards called iguanas that live in Mexico and in

Central America. He looked at Mantell's fossil teeth and told the doctor that they were just like iguana teeth, only much, much bigger.

Mantell was excited. It seemed to him that at one time there must have been huge lizards, giant iguanas, living in the world, and he had found some of their teeth. Since he had discovered this new animal, it was his right to name it. He called it *Iguanodon* (ih GWAHN uh dahn), which means "iguana tooth."

Scientists and other fossil hunters soon learned of Dr. Mantell's discovery. And, at just about the same time, another strange fossil was found—a huge jaw filled with sharp teeth. Scientists could tell that it was a jaw of a huge reptile. They named the reptile *Megalosaurus* (mehg uh luh SAWR uhs), meaning "giant lizard."

The teeth of *Iguanodon* show that this animal was a plant-eater. The teeth of *Megalosaurus* show that it was a meat-eater. Scientists could tell from the rocks the fossils were found in that the two animals had lived at about the same time. Scientists now realized for the first time that there had been giant reptiles living on earth millions of years ago—creatures no one had known about before and that weren't like anything living in the present-day world.

They were so big they must have been very terrible creatures. And it was thought that they were all a kind of lizard. So scientists took the Greek word *deinos*, meaning "terrible," and *sauros*, meaning "lizard," and put them together to make the word *dinosaur* (DY nuh sawr) or "terrible lizard."

All the dinosaurs had disappeared about sixty-five million years ago. Now these fantastic animals were once again known to the world.

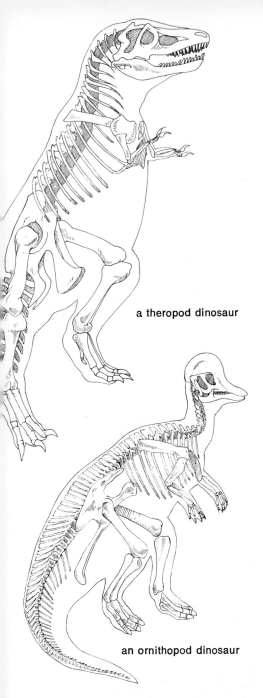

a theropod dinosaur

an ornithopod dinosaur

Meet the dinosaurs

What *was* a dinosaur?

Dinosaurs were a group of specialized reptiles that lived on land during most of the Age of Reptiles. *Dinosaur* is a name that means "terrible lizard." And many people have the idea that dinosaurs were a kind of giant lizard, but that's wrong. All dinosaurs weren't giants. Some dinosaurs were small. And dinosaurs weren't lizards. Lizards are one type of reptile; dinosaurs are another type of reptile.

There were six different "families" of dinosaurs. One family is called sauropods (SAWR uh pahdz), meaning "reptile-footed" dinosaurs. They were the biggest of the dinosaurs. All of these giant, four-footed plant-eaters had long necks and long tails. Another family was the theropods (THIHR uh pahdz), or "beast-footed" dinosaurs. All the theropods were meat-eaters that walked on two feet.

There were also ornithopods (AWR nuh

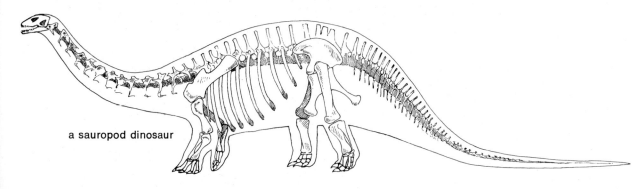

a sauropod dinosaur

a plated dinosaur

thuh pahdz), or "bird-footed" dinosaurs. They were plant-eaters that moved on two legs.

Two other families were the "armored" dinosaurs and "plated" dinosaurs. These two kinds of plant-eaters had bumpy, bone-covered skin and walked on all four feet. The ceratopsians (sehr uh TAPH see uhns), a name that means "horned faces," were among the last dinosaurs to appear. They, too, moved about on all four feet.

Dinosaurs were different in many ways. But they were all alike in a way that made them different from all other reptiles. A dinosaur's body was built for walking on two legs. There are no such reptiles in the world today.

An animal that walks on two legs is called a biped. And all the first dinosaurs were bipeds. They walked on their back legs. Later, some kinds of dinosaurs did get down and walk on all fours—but they still had the bodies of bipeds.

So that's what dinosaurs were— several different kinds of reptiles with bodies built for walking on two legs.

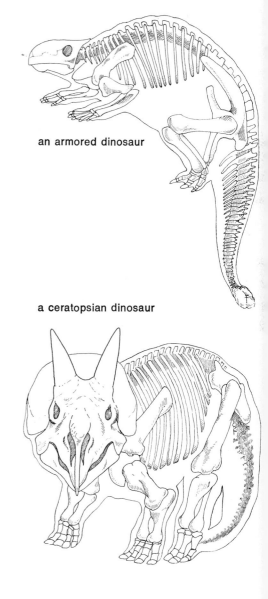

an armored dinosaur

a ceratopsian dinosaur

Look Alikes
Birds such as herons (above) look a little like the early dinosaur *Coelophysis* (below).

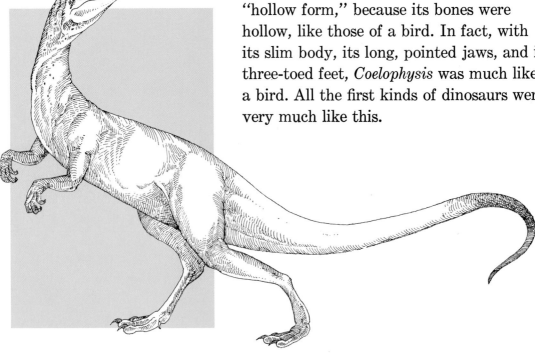

The first dinosaurs

The small, four-footed reptile was in a race for its life. Close behind it was a larger reptile, running on its two back legs. Its body was bent forward, its long neck and tail were stretched straight out.

With a sudden lunge of its head, the two-legged reptile caught the four-legged reptile in its long jaws. With its two front legs, it reached up and grasped the little animal in claws that looked like hands with four fingers. Holding the animal in these claws, it bit into it with sharp little teeth.

The two-legged reptile was one of the first kinds of dinosaurs. It lived about two hundred million years ago. A small animal, only about three feet (1 meter) high, it has the name *Coelophysis* (see LOH fuh sihs), or "hollow form," because its bones were hollow, like those of a bird. In fact, with its slim body, its long, pointed jaws, and its three-toed feet, *Coelophysis* was much like a bird. All the first kinds of dinosaurs were very much like this.

Becoming giants

Some of the dinosaurs were the biggest animals that ever walked the earth. They were enormous plant-eaters that walked on four feet. But the first dinosaurs were all little meat-eaters that walked around on two feet. Where, then, did all the great big plant-eaters come from?

Some of the little meat-eaters began to eat plants. Slowly, some of their descendants became animals that ate plants only. Some plant-eating dinosaurs remained small, but others became very large and could eat leaves from very high branches.

One of the first kinds of plant-eating dinosaurs was *Plateosaurus* (plat ee uh SAWR uhs). It was given this name, which means "broad lizard," because it had a bulky body. About twenty-one feet (6.3 meters) long, *Plateosaurus* often walked on its two back legs, like most early dinosaurs. But its front legs were nearly as thick and strong as its back ones. This shows that it often got down on all fours, probably to eat.

Slowly, the plant-eating dinosaurs such as *Plateosaurus* were turning into giants. And they were beginning to walk on all fours. In time, their descendants became enormous, four-footed plant-eaters.

Plateosaurus

The world of the dinosaurs

The air was hot and moist. Among the rushes that crowded the edge of a great river, hundreds of frogs croaked at one another. On the muddy shore, some crocodiles lay sleeping. A turtle plodded slowly by them, slipped into the water, and swam on its way. There was a rumble of thunder. Lightning flickered in the gray sky. Rain came spattering down on the still water of the river.

Standing some distance from shore, were a number of enormous creatures. They had long, snakelike necks and tails, huge bodies, and legs the size of tree trunks. Their skins shimmered wetly in the rain. Except for the slow turnings of their tiny heads, they seemed motionless. They were sauropod dinosaurs called *Apatosaurus* (ap uh tuh SAWR uhs).

The rain hissed down onto the forest that spread

out on all sides of the river. It rattled sharply on the fan-shaped leaves of the ginkgo trees and dripped from the tall palms. Through the wet underbrush came a long-tailed *Ornitholestes* (awr nuh thuh LEHS teez), about the size of a young child. It trotted along with quick little birdlike steps. Suddenly it paused and cocked an eye at a clump of ferns. Then it darted forward. A tiny, furry, ratlike animal hidden among the ferns tried to scurry to safety. But it was too slow. It squealed in terror as the reptile seized it.

Elsewhere in the forest a *Camptosaurus* (kamp tuh SAWR uhs), a two-legged reptile somewhat taller

(continued from page 122)

than a tall man, plodded among the dripping trees.
Spying a small cluster of low-growing leafy plants, it
got down on all fours and began to eat.

There was a sound of slow, heavy footsteps. The
Camptosaurus lifted its head, its body tense, ready to
run if the sounds meant danger.

A huge, bulky, four-legged creature came trudging
through the forest. Its back legs were much longer
than its front ones. So, while its small, birdlike head

nearly touched the ground, its hips were higher than its head. Along this creature's back ran a double row of large, flat, skin-covered pieces of bone, shaped like upside-down hearts. Its long, powerful tail projected above the ground behind it. At the end of its tail were four long, sharp spikes of bone, like horns.

The *Camptosaurus* went back to its feeding. This big creature, a *Stegosaurus* (stehg uh SAWR uhs), was a plant-eater. It was no threat. It clumped on into the forest and was soon out of sight.

(continued on page 127)

(continued from page 125)

Before long, the rain passed over. Beams of sunlight now slanted down among the trees. Finishing its meal of leaves, the *Camptosaurus* stood up. Once again it moved through the forest, searching for more of the leafy plants that were its main food. Shortly, it found some, growing thickly near a dark, shadowy part of the forest. Once more it got down on all fours to eat.

From out of the shadows, where it had squatted in hiding, rushed a huge, fearsome reptile—an *Allosaurus* (al uh SAWR uhs). This great beast had a big head and a grinning mouth full of sharp, savage teeth. It ran on two legs, bent over, with its tail stretched straight out behind it. In three strides it was upon the plant-eater. Its great jaws closed on the smaller reptile's neck, killing it instantly.

Hungrily, the huge meat-eater began to feed. It bent forward, the claws on its front legs resting on the dead plant-eater's body. With a twist of its head, it tore off a great chunk of flesh.

When the meat-eater had had its fill, it rose up on its hind legs and stalked off into the forest. It would soon find a sheltered place to squat down and sleep. When it awoke, it would hunt again.

This was the world of the dinosaurs, 140 million years ago. Dinosaurs much like these lived in all parts of the world. Their ways of life were not really at all different from the ways the animals of today live. Plant-eating dinosaurs probably spent much of their time eating, just as zebras, gazelles, and most other plant-eaters do now. Meat-eating dinosaurs probably acted much the same way lions and tigers do now. For, although dinosaurs seem strange to us, they were simply another sort of animal.

The giant plant-eaters

The biggest of all the dinosaurs were the long-necked, plant-eating dinosaurs called sauropods (SAWR uh pahdz), which means "lizard-footed." Some of these dinosaurs were the biggest animals that have ever lived on the land.

There were many kinds of sauropods. One of the best known is *Apatosaurus* (ap uh tuh SAWR uhs). The name *Apatosaurus* means something like "untrue lizard." It may have been given this name because the man who found its fossil bones couldn't believe that such a huge creature was real.

These animals were sixty to eighty feet (18 to 24 meters) long. They probably weighed thirty tons (27 metric tons) or more. When such an enormous, heavy animal walked, it must have sounded like distant thunder! So *Apatosaurus* is also called *Brontosaurus* (brahn tuh SAWR uhs), or "thunder lizard."

Diplodocus (duh PLAHD uh kuhs) was even longer than *Apatosaurus*—ninety feet (27 meters) from its nose to the tip of its tail. But it was not as bulky and heavy as *Apatosaurus*. *Diplodocus* means "double beam," a name that refers to the way part of this animal's skeleton is formed.

One of the biggest and heaviest of all the sauropods, *Brachiosaurus* (brak ee uh SAWR uhs), could have looked over the top of a three-story building! It was about seventy

The fossil skeleton of an *Apatosaurus.*

130

(continued from page 128)

to eighty feet (21 to 24 meters) long. But its head
was just about forty feet (12 meters) above the
ground. A big *Brachiosaurus* weighed about fifty
tons (45 metric tons), or about as much as seven big
elephants! This animal's name means "upper-arm
lizard," and comes from the fact that its front legs
were longer than its back ones. These sauropods
were among the biggest animals that ever
lived on land. A huge *Ultrasaurus* (uhl truh SAWR
uhs) has been discovered that must have been more
than 100 feet (30 meters) long. *Ultrasaurus* means
something like "the greatest possible lizard." And
maybe Ultrasaurus wasn't quite the "greatest
possible" dinosaur. Recently scientists have
discovered even larger and heavier sauropods. Who
knows what the final record will show!

Another sauropod dinosaur was *Camarasaurus*
(kam uh ruh SAWR uhs). The name *Camarasaurus*
means "vaulted-arch lizard," referring to part of the
animal's skeleton. *Camarasaurus* was some sixty or
more feet (18 meters) long. However, one skeleton of
a young *Camarasaurus* was found that was only
about sixteen feet (4.8 meters) long. This "baby"
sauropod died, or was killed, before it grew up.

There were many other kinds of sauropods, all with
long necks, long tails, bulky bodies, and thick legs.
Sauropod dinosaurs lived all over the world, from 150
million to about 70 million years ago. Some of them
may have lived even later.

For a long time it was thought that sauropods
probably spent most of their time wading in swamps
and streams, because most sauropods had nostrils on
the tops of their heads.

Now most scientists think that the sauropod dinosaurs may have roamed the plains in herds, much as elephants do. And they may have used their long necks to reach up to get tender leaves and buds from the tops of trees, just as giraffes do. Perhaps the sauropods were so big that meat-eaters hesitated to attack them, just as lions and tigers will not attack elephants. If so, meat-eating dinosaurs may have feasted only on dead sauropods.

We are still learning more about these strange, big animals. Perhaps, someday, we will know for sure just how they lived.

Diplodocus

The small meat-eaters

Sharp teeth, claws like daggers, and front feet that looked like hands. These were the main features of most of the dinosaurs that are called theropods (THIHR uh pahdz). *Theropod* means "beast-foot." The theropods were sharp-toothed meat-eaters that stalked their prey on two legs!

Many theropods probably got their food by running after it. The small theropods were probably quite fast. They had slim, light bodies, and hollow bones, just as birds do. In many ways, these dinosaurs were a lot like birds, with long, slender jaws and birdlike legs.

One of the small theropods was the smallest of all the dinosaurs. It was no bigger than a turkey. It is called *Compsognathus* (kahmp SAHG nuh thuhs), which means "graceful jaw." *Compsognathus* probably scurried about on the shores of lagoons or the banks of rivers, chasing insects, smaller reptiles, and amphibians for food.

A little bigger theropod was *Ornitholestes* (awr nuh thuh LEHS teez), which means "bird catcher." It was about three feet (1 meter) high. It, too, got its food by chasing smaller creatures. After catching an animal, *Ornitholestes* may have used its three-fingered claws to hold the animal while eating it. Both *Ornitholestes* and *Compsognathus* lived about 150 million to 130 million years ago.

Bigger still, and perhaps a great deal more fierce, was a theropod called *Deinonychus* (dy NAHN ee kuhs). The name means "terrible claw." And this animal does seem to have been a terrible creature for its size. It was only about five feet (1.5 meters) high. But it had sharp, sawlike teeth, and curved, sharp claws on its "hands"

Compsognathus

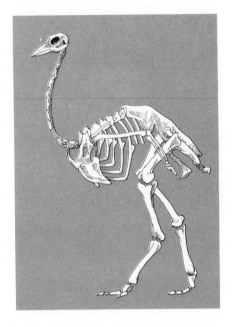

Look Alikes

The ostrich of today (above), is much like the dinosaur called *Struthiomimus* (below).

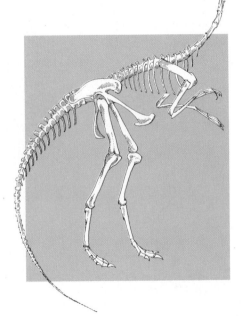

(continued from page 132)

and feet. One claw on each foot was very large, and was a special kind of weapon. *Deinonychus* must have been able to kick out with its feet, using these terrible claws like slashing swords. It was probably able to attack animals that were a little bigger than it was. *Deinonychus* lived about one hundred million years ago.

One kind of small theropod must have looked more like a big ostrich than like a reptile. It is named *Struthiomimus* (stroo thee oh MY muhs), or "ostrich imitator." Except for its long tail, the fossil skeleton of this dinosaur looks very much like the skeleton of an ostrich. Its skull resembles that of an ostrich. And, like an ostrich, it had toothless jaws covered with a bill. It was even about the same size as an ostrich —eight feet (2.4 meters) high.

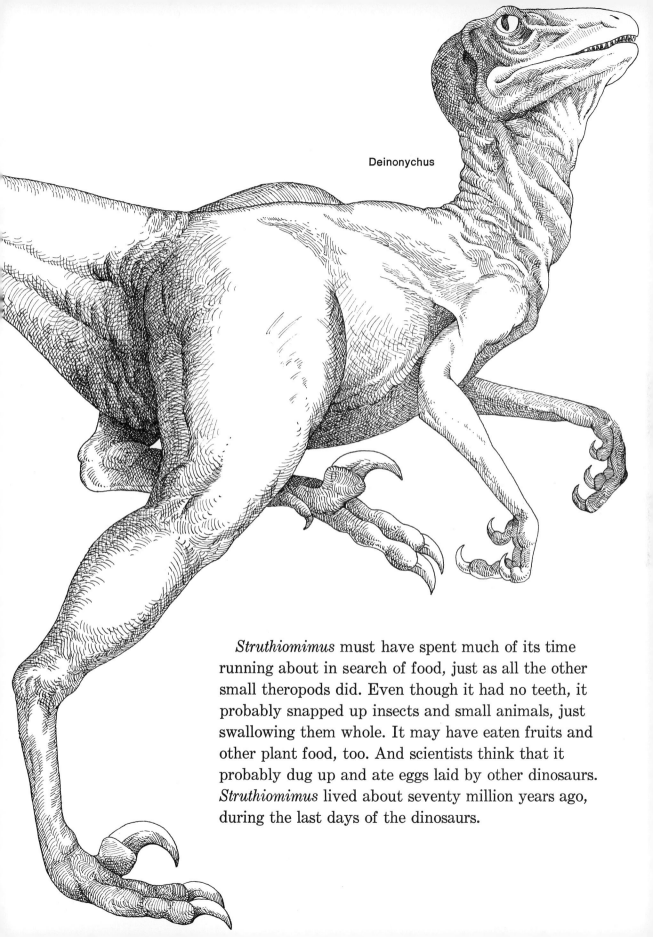

Deinonychus

Struthiomimus must have spent much of its time running about in search of food, just as all the other small theropods did. Even though it had no teeth, it probably snapped up insects and small animals, just swallowing them whole. It may have eaten fruits and other plant food, too. And scientists think that it probably dug up and ate eggs laid by other dinosaurs. *Struthiomimus* lived about seventy million years ago, during the last days of the dinosaurs.

The giant meat-eaters

The still waters of the broad lake shimmered in the moonlight. The scene looked peaceful and quiet. But along the shore, a huge, hungry animal was hunting. It stalked rapidly along on its two big hind legs, leaving three-toed footprints in the mud. Its head was as big as a barrel and its teeth were like long, sharp knife blades. This terror of the forest was a fearsome sight. It was a giant, flesh-eating theropod dinosaur!

The giant theropods were different from the small theropods in several ways. Instead of having long, slender necks, their necks were short and thick. And instead of having birdlike heads, with jaws like beaks, their heads were huge.

One of the first of the giant meat-eating theropods is called *Teratosaurus* (tehr uh tuh SAWR uhs), which is a name that means "monster lizard." Only about twenty feet (6 meters) long, it was a rather small giant. But it was one of the biggest beasts of prey of its time. It had strong front legs, with three claws on each foot. It may have used these claws to hold animals while it killed them with a bite of its big jaws. *Teratosaurus* lived about 190 million years ago.

Later there were many kinds of giant theropods, all bigger than *Teratosaurus*. *Allosaurus* (al uh SAWR uhs), or "other lizard," roamed the plains and swamps 150 million years ago. It was about thirty feet (9 meters) long and ten feet (3 meters) high.

Giant theropods such as *Allosaurus* ate big animals, such as the huge, plant-eating sauropod dinosaur *Apatosaurus* (also called *Brontosaurus*). Several fossil bones of *Apatosaurus* have been

Tyrannosaurus

The fossil skeleton of an *Allosaurus*.

(continued from page 136)

found with *Allosaurus* teeth marks in them! When an *Allosaurus* fed on such creatures, it tore huge chunks out of their bodies and swallowed these down at one gulp, without chewing!

As time went on, many other kinds of giant theropods

appeared. About a hundred million years ago there were two big theropods called *Albertosaurus* (al bur tuh SAWR uhs) and *Spinosaurus* (spyn uh SAWR uhs).

Albertosaurus, or "Alberta lizard," lived in what is now Alberta, Canada. This meat-eater was thirty-five feet (10.5 meters) long, but its front legs were tiny and there were only two "fingers" on its "hands."

Spinosaurus means "spined lizard." This creature had a big fin sticking up out of its backbone. Scientists do not know what this big fin was for.

Finally, about seventy million years ago, there lived the biggest theropod of all—*Tyrannosaurus rex* (tih ran uh SAWR uhs rehks), a name meaning "tyrant king lizard." *Tyrannosaurus* was the biggest meat-eating animal that has ever walked the earth. Some of the tyrannosaurs were nearly fifty feet (15 meters) long and eighteen feet (5.4 meters) high! And these creatures had heads that were nearly as long as a man's whole body. Their daggerlike teeth were six inches (15 centimeters) long.

Albertosaurus and *Tyrannosaurus* may have been too big and heavy to run long distances after their prey, as the smaller theropods did. These huge monsters probably stalked the dinosaurs they wanted to eat, and then rushed at them over a short distance. However, there are some scientists who think that *Albertosaurus* and *Tyrannosaurus* weren't hunters at all. It is possible that they only ate the bodies of dead dinosaurs they found as they prowled about the great swamps and forests.

There were also other kinds of giant theropods in addition to the ones named here. They lived in all parts of the world during most of the 130 million years that dinosaurs ruled the earth.

The plated dinosaurs

Some dinosaurs were protected by many flat, hard pieces of bone on their bodies. Because of these bones, called plates, these animals are called plated dinosaurs.

The first plated dinosaur we know of lived about 170 million years ago, where England is today. It was a plant-eater, with a bulky body, four thick legs, and a small head. This animal is named *Scelidosaurus* (sehl uh duh SAWR uhs), or "side lizard," because of the rows of bony bumps running down its back and sides.

Scelidosaurus wasn't very big—only about

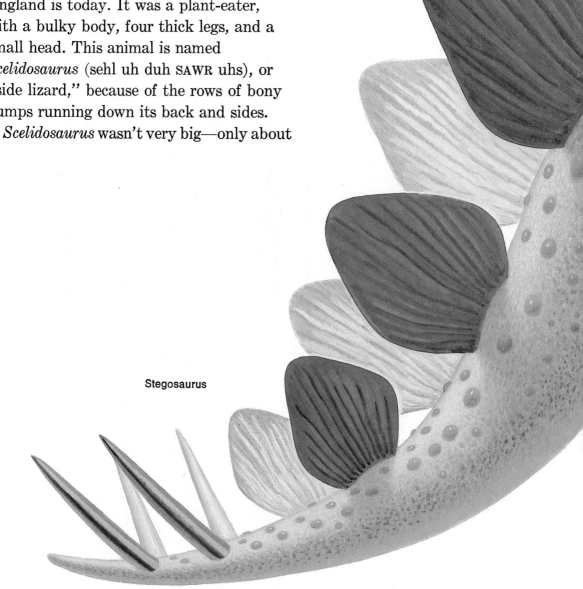

Stegosaurus

(continued from page 140)

twelve feet (3.6 meters) long. But as millions of years went by, plated dinosaurs got bigger and bigger.

One plated dinosaur, *Stegosaurus* (stehg uh SAWR uhs), was surely one of the strangest-looking of all dinosaurs. *Stegosaurus* was about twenty-five feet (7.5 meters) long. Its back legs were much longer than its front legs. Because of this, its little head was close to the ground, while its hips were the highest part of its body. Up its back and down its tail ran two rows of huge plates shaped like triangles. And on the end of its tail were two pair of big, sharp spikes. Each spike was nearly two feet (0.6 meter) long.

Stegosaurus means "roofed lizard." The animal was given this name because the plates sticking up from its back look much like old-fashioned roof shingles. Scientists think these hard, pointed plates might have kept meat-eating dinosaurs from jumping on the back of a *Stegosaurus*. As for its spiky tail, *Stegosaurus* probably used it like a war club. Swung hard at a meat-eater, this tail would be a real weapon. The four sharp spikes would have made terrible wounds in a meat-eater's body.

Stegosaurus lived in North America, but other kinds of plated dinosaurs very much like it lived in other parts of the world. One of these, *Kentrosaurus* (kehn truh SAWR uhs), had plates running partway up its back, and seven pair of sharp spikes running from its hips down its tail.

Some dinosaurs did not become extinct until about sixty-five million years ago, but the plated dinosaurs all died out earlier—about 80 million years ago. Their place in the dinosaur world was taken over by the armored dinosaurs.

The armored dinosaurs

Plodding through the tall, grasslike plants of a broad plain came an animal that was like a living tank! Its blunt head and broad body were covered with thick, bumpy, bony armor. Its tail, as thick as a young tree trunk, was tipped with a huge, heavy knob of bone, studded with bony spikes.

Suddenly, the animal stopped. It had caught sight of another creature hurrying toward it—a two-legged creature with a big head, and jaws filled with sharp teeth. A meat-eater! At once, the armored reptile crouched down, pulling its legs beneath its body and lowering its head.

The huge *Tyrannosaurus*, was fiercely hungry. But even its sharp teeth and strong jaws could

Palaeoscincus, an armored dinosaur, and the flesh-eater *Tyrannosaurus.*

(continued from page 143)

not bite through the thick, bony armor of the crouching reptile. Angrily, the *Tyrannosaurus* lashed out with a great clawed foot, pushing at the armored creature, trying to turn it over.

It was a bad mistake for the *Tyrannosaurus*. The armored creature swiftly swung its tail. The heavy club of bone smashed into the *Tyrannosaurus'* leg. The meat-eater staggered back and fell to the ground, its leg shattered by the armored dinosaur's clublike tail!

With their bony armor and war-club tails, armored dinosaurs were probably able to protect themselves from the teeth of meat-eaters. Most armored dinosaurs were bulky beasts, twelve to fifteen feet (3.6 to 4.5 meters) long and four to five feet (1.2 to 1.5 meters) high. All were plant-eaters, with small, weak teeth and could chew only soft plants.

Hylaeosaurus

One of the first armored dinosaurs lived about 130 million years ago. It is called *Pinacosaurus* (pin acko SAWR uhs), a name that refers to its long tail. This dinosaur had bumps of bone sticking up all over its body. At the end of its long tail was a big clump of bone shaped somewhat like the head of an ax!

Acanthopholis (uh kan thuh FOH lihs), which means "thorn-scale covered," lived a few million years after *Pinacosaurus*. It had rows of sharp spikes and bony plates on its back. *Hylaeosaurus* (hy lee uh SAWR uhs), or "forest lizard," had a double row of spikes running down its back, and another double row of spikes down its tail.

Armored dinosaurs that lived later had even heavier armor. One of these dinosaurs was *Palaeoscincus* (pay lee uh SKINK uhs), or "ancient skink" (a skink is a kind of lizard). It lived about eighty million years ago. Its back was covered by a solid shield of bony plates.

Ankylosaurus (ang kuh luh SAWR uhs), or "stiff lizard," was an armored dinosaur that lived about seventy million years ago. It was almost completely covered by bony armor.

The armor of these creatures wasn't stiff, like the shell of a turtle, but was actually movable, much like the bony armor of an armadillo of today.

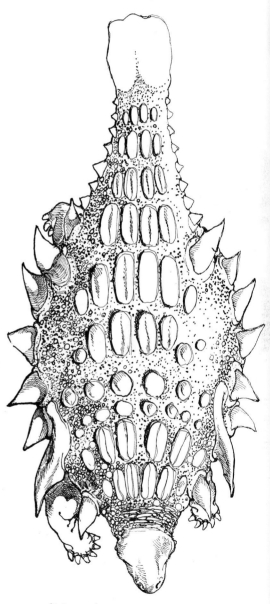

Palaeoscincus

Bird-footed and bone-headed dinosaurs

"Duck-billed" dinosaurs, and dinosaurs with spikes for "thumbs"! These creatures belonged to the group of dinosaurs called ornithopods (AWR nuh thuh pahdz), meaning "bird-footed."

All the first kinds of ornithopods were rather small reptiles that walked on two legs. One of them, called *Camptosaurus* (kamp tuh SAWR uhs), or "bent lizard," lived about 150 million years ago. It was only about fifteen feet (4.5 meters) long. Although it walked on its two hind legs, its front legs were stout, with broad "hands." This means that *Camptosaurus* probably spent a lot of time on all fours, feeding on low-growing plants.

Later, about 125 million years ago, there was a much bigger ornithopod called *Iguanodon* (ih GWAHN uh dahn). *Iguanodon* means "iguana tooth."

Iguanodon was much like *Camptosaurus*, but much bigger and more bulky—about thirty feet (9 meters) long. *Iguanodon* was also different from *Camptosaurus* in one special way—the "thumbs" on its "hands" were big sharp spikes! Perhaps *Iguanodon* used these spikes to fight off attacks of meat-eating dinosaurs that were looking for a meal.

Camptosaurus

About ninety million years ago, there were several kinds of rather strange creatures that are often called "bone-headed" dinosaurs. One of them is named *Pachycephalosaurus* (pak uh sehf uh luh SAWR uhs), which means "thick-headed lizard."

About the same size and shape as *Iguanodon*, this dinosaur had six small, blunt horns on its nose and a

(continued from page 147)
cluster of spiky bumps on the back of its head. And the top of its head was a big, hard bump of bone some ten inches (25 centimeters) thick!

Scientists aren't exactly sure why the top of its skull was so thick. Perhaps these dinosaurs used their thick skulls as weapons. They may have fought with each other by banging their heads together, the way goats and sheep do today.

Iguanodon

The duckbilled dinosaurs

About seventy million years ago, a group of dinosaurs trooped out of a forest onto the bank of a broad river. They were big reptiles that walked on two legs. Their heads looked strangely like the head of a duck, for their jaws were covered by a bill, much like a duck's bill.

Suddenly, the creatures stopped. Their heads lifted, as if they heard or smelled something. Quickly, they plunged into the water. With only their heads and backs above water, they looked like huge, swimming ducks, with scaly skins instead of feathers.

These creatures are called duckbilled dinosaurs because of their ducklike jaws. They were part of the ornithopod, or "bird-footed," group of dinosaurs. There were many kinds of duckbilled dinosaurs that lived from about one hundred million to seventy million years ago. They were all plant-eaters that may have spent much of their time in and around rivers.

(continued on page 152)

Anatosaurus

Look Alikes

The dinosaur *Corythosaurus* (above) had a bony crest on its head, much like that of the bird called a cassowary (below).

(continued from page 151)
The fossils of duckbills show that they had webbed feet and tails that were flattened at the sides. This means that they were good swimmers.

All duckbilled dinosaurs had several rows of teeth, packed closely together, in both their upper and lower jaws. Thus a duckbill might have as many as two thousand teeth! All these teeth formed a rough, bumpy surface. The duckbills ground the tough plants they ate between these bunches of teeth. Of course, all that grinding made the teeth wear down. But as one set of teeth wore out, these dinosaurs grew another set to take its place!

Most of the duckbills had strange kinds of bony "ornaments" on their heads. One, *Lambeosaurus* (lam bee uh SAWR uhs), named for a scientist, had a bony shape that looked like an ax sticking up out of its head! And *Corythosaurus* (kuh rihth uh SAWR uhs), or "helmeted lizard," had a flat half-circle of bone that was like part of an old-fashioned helmet.

Cheneosaurus (kee nee uh SAWR uhs), or "goose lizard," had a bump of bone on its forehead. And *Gryposaurus* (grihp uh SAWR uhs), the "hook-nosed lizard," had a bony bump on its nose. But strangest of all was *Parasaurolophus* (par uh sawr AWL uh fuhs), or "near lizard with a crest." This animal had a long, curved tube of bone sticking out of the top of its head.

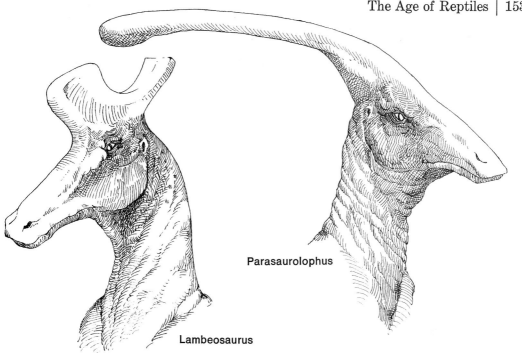

Parasaurolophus

Lambeosaurus

Scientists aren't sure what all these bumps, tubes, and crests were for. But one idea is that the ornaments may have helped duckbills to recognize others of their own kind.

However, most of the bony ornaments were hollow and contained passages that were connected to the animals' noses. So, these ornaments could have been noise-makers! The duckbills may have made hooting and honking sounds to attract mates. The differently shaped ornaments could have helped make different sounds. Thus, each kind of duckbill may have had its own mating call, according to the shape of its head ornament.

Most of the duckbills were large dinosaurs. One of the biggest, *Anatosaurus* (uh nat uh SAWR uhs), the "ducklike lizard," was thirty feet (9 meters) long and eighteen feet (5.4 meters) high. *Anatosaurus* did not have a bony formation on its head. For that reason, it is often called a "flat-headed" duckbill.

The horned dinosaurs

When duckbilled dinosaurs and huge tyrannosaurs roamed and prowled the earth, there were also several kinds of dinosaurs with snouts like a parrot's beak and horns on their heads. These dinosaurs are known as ceratopsians (sehr uh TAHPS ee uhns), which means "horned faces."

The horned dinosaurs were about the last kind of dinosaur to come into the world. These animals walked on four legs, but they were probably descended from dinosaurs that walked on two legs.

About one hundred million years ago, in what is now Mongolia, there was a small ceratopsian we call *Protoceratops* (proh toh SEHR uh tahps). Its name means "first horned face." *Protoceratops* wasn't really the first of the horned dinosaurs, but it was probably very much like they must have been.

Protoceratops was about six feet (1.8 meters) long. It had a nose shaped like a parrot's beak. It also had a kind of bony shield that grew out of the back of its skull and covered its neck. All ceratopsians had this kind of shield. But *Protoceratops*, although it was a ceratopsian, did not have any horns—only a sort of bump on its nose.

By about ninety million years ago, there were several different kinds of much bigger, truly horned dinosaurs. *Monoclonius* (mahn uh KLOH nee uhs), which means something like "single horn," was about seventeen feet (5.1 meters) long and seven feet (2.1 meters) high. It had a long, sharp horn on its nose. *Styracosaurus* (sty rak uh SAWR uhs), or "spiked lizard," had a long horn on its nose, too—but it also had six horns coming out of its bony head shield!

The fossil skull of a
Triceratops, one of
the horned dinosaurs.

Later—about eighty million years ago—there lived
Pentaceratops (pehn tuh SEHR uh tahps), which means
"five-horned face." This dinosaur had a short horn on
its nose, a pair of long horns above its eyes, and a horn
sticking out on each of its cheeks. It was a little bigger
than *Styracosaurus* and *Monoclonius*.

Living at the same time as *Pentaceratops* was a
"horned" dinosaur that had no horn. This creature is
called *Pachyrhinosaurus* (pak uh ryn uh SAWR uhs),
meaning "thick-nosed lizard." Instead of a horn on its
nose, it had a big, rough sort of knob of bone. These
dinosaurs may have used their bony bumps to fight

Monoclonius

(continued from page 155)
each other, bumping their heads together the same
way goats do.

One of the last and largest of the ceratopsians was
Triceratops (try SEHR uh tahps), or "three-horned
face." It had a short horn on its nose and a long horn
above each eye. *Triceratops* lived seventy million
years ago and was more than twenty feet (6 meters)
long.

The ceratopsians ate plants. They may have been
attacked by the big meat-eating dinosaurs, such as

Tyrannosaurus

Albertosaurus and *Tyrannosaurus*. However, most ceratopsians could have defended themselves quite well, especially when traveling in herds. Groups of monocloniuses could have charged an attacker and stabbed it with their horns.

Centrosaurus (sehn truh SAWR uhs), or "sharp-pointed lizard," was closely related to *Monoclonius*. *Centrosaurus* was about twenty feet (6 meters) long and had a nose horn that was bent forward. Some scientists think that *Centrosaurus* was really another kind of *Monoclonius*.

Reptiles of the sea

Dinosaurs "ruled" the land for millions of years. But during this time, many other kinds of reptiles lived on the land and in the seas.

The sea reptiles were air-breathing animals whose ancestors had been land creatures. But now their legs had become flippers and they spent their lives in water. Many of these reptiles were as huge as some of the large dinosaurs.

One group of sea reptiles looked almost exactly like big fish. These were the ichthyosaurs (IHK thee uh sawrz), a name that means "fish-lizard." They had fish-shaped bodies, with four flippers on their undersides and a large fin on the back. However, their jaws were much like the jaws of long-snouted crocodiles—long and thin, with sharp teeth. Most ichthyosaurs were from eight to ten feet (2.4 to 3 meters) long, but some were more than twice that size.

Ichthyosaurs probably lived much the same way dolphins do now. They swam like most fish do, by wiggling their tails. They used their flippers to steer with. Most of them ate fish, and a few kinds ate small cephalopods. Unlike sea reptiles of today, such as sea turtles, ichthyosaurs did not come onto land to lay eggs. Their babies were born in the water.

Another group of sea reptiles were the plesiosaurs (PLEE see uh sawrz), or "near lizards." There were two kinds—long-necked and short-necked. A long-necked plesiosaur had a bulky body with four big flippers, like paddles. It also had a short, pointed tail and a small head on a long neck. Its neck was often longer than its whole body!

The long-necked plesiosaurs that lived about 150

plesiosaurs

million years ago were from ten to twenty feet (3 to 6 meters) long. Those that lived later were often much longer. One, which lived about seventy million years ago, was more than forty feet (13.2 meters) long.

Instead of swimming like fish, as ichthyosaurs did, plesiosaurs swam by sort of rowing themselves along with their paddles. They seem to have eaten almost any small creature they could catch. In the fossil skeleton of one plesiosaur were the fossil remains of

Look Alikes

The modern dolphin (above) looks much like a prehistoric ichthyosaur (below).

(continued from page 159)

some of the things it had eaten—some fish, a small squid, and a small, winged reptile.

The short-necked plesiosaurs had bodies, flippers, and tails much like those of the long-necked plesiosaurs. But instead of having small heads on long necks, they had very large, long heads. One of them, found in Australia, was called *Kronosaurus* (krohn uh SAWR uhs), after the giant Greek god Kronos. Nearly fifty feet (15 meters) long, its head was so big that two tall men could have lain head to foot in its jaws!

Still another reptile that lived in the sea in the Age of Reptiles was the mosasaur (MOH suh sawr). It was given this name, which means "Meuse lizard," because its fossils were first found close to the Meuse River, in The Netherlands. Mosasaurs were lizards. They looked somewhat like big crocodiles with stretched-out bodies and flippers instead of legs. The biggest were about 35 feet (10.5 meters) long. These creatures ate fish and shellfish.

Other big reptiles swam in those long-ago seas, too—giant turtles and giant crocodiles. Reptiles ruled the seas during the Age of Reptiles, just as they ruled the land.

The flying reptiles

Above the waves that rolled in from the sea and surged up onto a sandy beach, a small flying creature soared. The creature's wings curved back into points, and a long, skinny tail stretched out behind it. Its head was birdlike, with long, slender jaws. But a bird has no teeth—and this animal had large, pointed teeth in its jaws. Skimming over the beach, the creature soared out of sight.

This strange kind of flying animal lived about 150 million years ago, at the same time as such dinosaurs as *Apatosaurus* and *Allosaurus*. It was not a bird. It was one of the group of creatures we call pterosaurs (TEHR uh sawrz), meaning "flying reptiles." It was given the name *Rhamphorhynchus* (ram fuh RIHNG kuhs), which means "prow-beak."

Rhamphorhynchus had a body about eighteen inches (45 centimeters) long. When it spread its wings, they stretched out about two feet (0.6 meter). Its wings were not at all like a bird's wings, with feathers. These wings were only thin pieces of skin. Yet this creature could probably fly very well by flapping its wings, just as a bird does. The end of this reptile's tail was flattened out into a kind of rounded paddle shape. *Rhamphorhynchus* probably used its tail to steer with while flying.

Scientists think that *Rhamphorhynchus* lived near water, swooping down to snatch up small fish in its toothy jaws. It probably spent a lot of time in trees.

There were many other kinds of pterosaurs living during the Age of Reptiles. *Dimorphodon* (dy MAWR fuh dahn), or "two shapes of teeth," which lived a little before *Rhamphorhynchus*, was bigger—about

(continued on page 165)

Rhamphorhynchus

Pterodactylus

Dimorphodon

Pteranodon

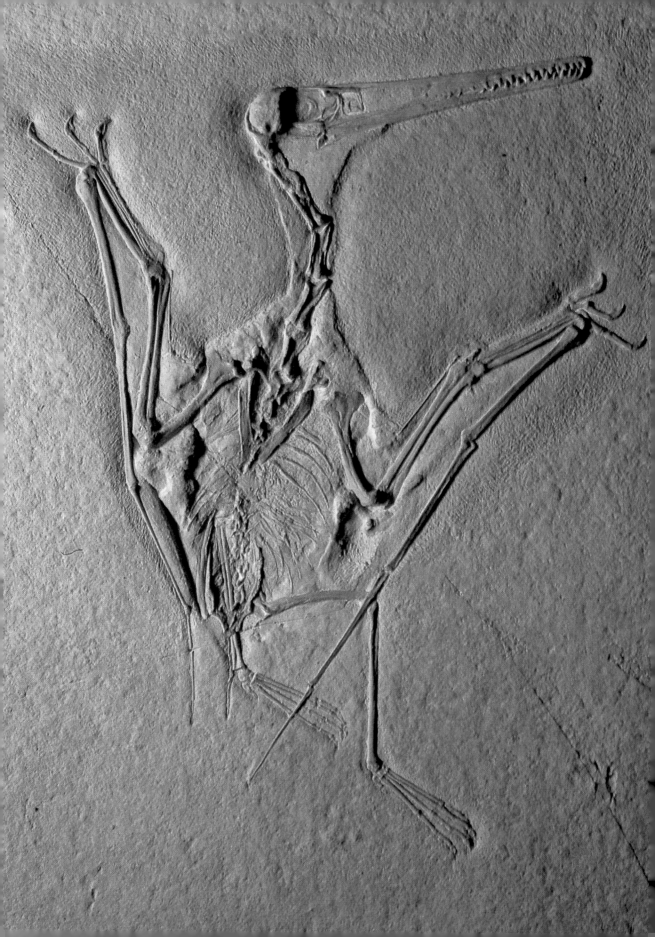

(continued from page 161)
three feet (1 meter) long. *Pterodactylus* (tehr uh DAK tuh luhs), or "winged-finger," which lived at about the same time as *Rhamphorhynchus,* was smaller—about the size of a sparrow. *Dimorphodon* had a long, thin tail, while *Pterodactylus* had hardly any tail at all.

There is one strange thing about these pterosaurs. Although they were reptiles, they didn't have a scaly skin, as do snakes, lizards, and other reptiles of today. Their bodies were covered with a kind of hair! There's no such thing as a hairy reptile now.

Near the end of the Age of Reptiles, there were some big pterosaurs. About eighty million years ago, there was a pterosaur called *Pteranodon* (tehr AN uh dahn), or "winged without teeth." It was only about the size of a goose, but its wings stretched more than twenty feet (6 meters) from tip to tip. And about seventy million years ago, there was a pterosaur that was probably the biggest flying creature that has ever lived. Its wings spread out to 51 feet (15.3 meters). That's longer than the wings of many small airplanes!

This giant pterosaur has been named *Quetzalcoatlus* (keht sahl koh AH tuhl uhs), after Quetzalcoatl, who was the feathered serpent-god of the ancient Aztec Indians. *Quetzalcoatlus* may have lived on fish, as the other pterosaurs did. But some scientists think it may have lived much like vultures do now, by eating the bodies of dead animals it found. Only the animals that *it* ate were dinosaurs!

The fossil skeleton of a *Pterodactylus.*

Reptiles with shells

People think of turtles as being rather stupid and slow. But actually, these creatures have done rather well. They have been in the world for more than two hundred million years. When the first small dinosaurs were scampering about in search of prey, there were already turtles around. Perhaps the turtles' shells protected them from the little dinosaurs.

The oldest kinds of turtles we know about weren't very different from today's turtles. They were small, slow-moving creatures with blunt heads, short tails, and bumpy shells. However, the first kinds of turtles had teeth in the roof of their mouth, and no turtle now

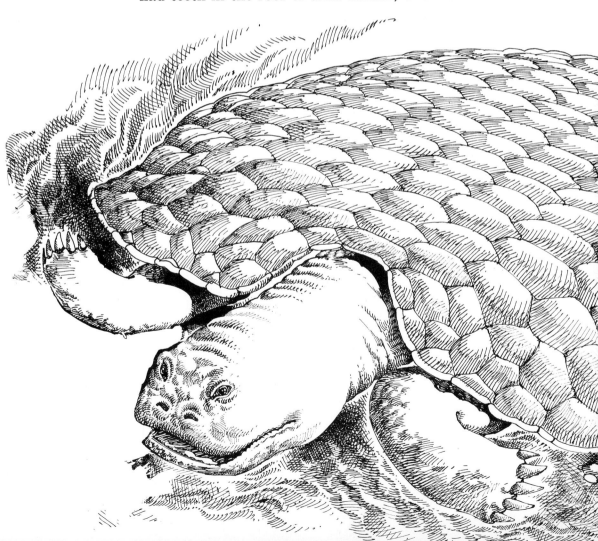

has teeth—their mouths are like a bird's beak. And the first kinds of turtles could not pull their heads, legs, and tails all the way into their shells, as most turtles can now.

Turtles are now the only reptiles that have shells. But at about the same time the first kinds of turtles were plodding about, there were also other kinds of reptiles with shells. About two hundred million years ago, in what is now Germany, there were some reptiles with square-shaped heads and broad, flat shells that were like big, shallow, upside-down soup bowls. These creatures had only one tooth on each side of the lower jaw. They have been named *Henodus* (HEHN uh duhs), meaning "single tooth."

(continued on page 168)

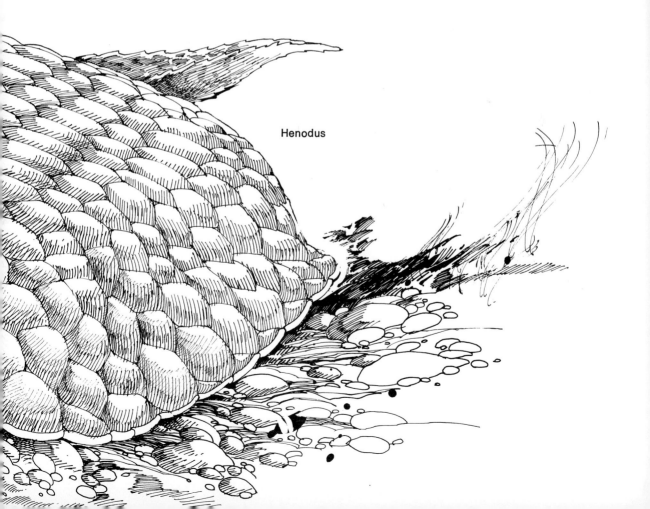

Henodus

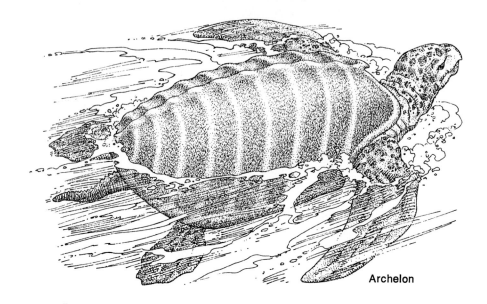

Archelon

(continued from page 167)

Henodus was a water reptile that probably lived along seacoasts and ate shellfish. It was about five feet (1.3 meters) long. Although it looked much like some kind of turtle, it was not related to the turtle group at all.

Henodus became extinct, but turtles increased. The first kinds of turtles probably lived near ponds and streams and spent some of their time in water. Later, some kinds of turtles took to the sea. And some of them became giants! A turtle called *Archelon* (AHR kuh lahn), or "king turtle," that lived about seventy million years ago was the biggest turtle that ever lived. It was about twelve feet (3.6 meters) long and eleven feet (3.3 meters) wide. *Archelon* lived in the great sea that covered most of North America during the Age of Reptiles.

The fossil skeleton of a giant turtle of about eighty million years ago.

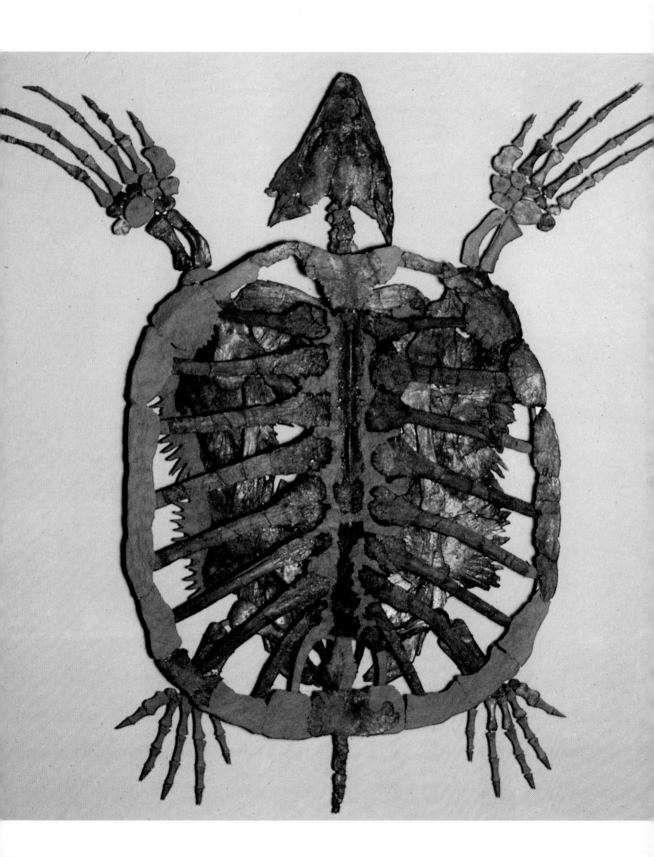

A borrowed way of life

A crocodile is a copycat! It's imitating another kind of reptile that swam in lakes and streams two hundred million years ago!

The reptile that crocodiles are copying is called a phytosaur (FY tuh sawr), which means "plant-eating lizard." But that name is a mistake, because we now know that it was a meat-eater—and probably a fierce one. Some phytosaurs were as much as fifteen feet

Look Alikes
The gavial (right), as well as the crocodile and alligator, are all very much like the phytosaur (below), a reptile of two hundred million years ago.

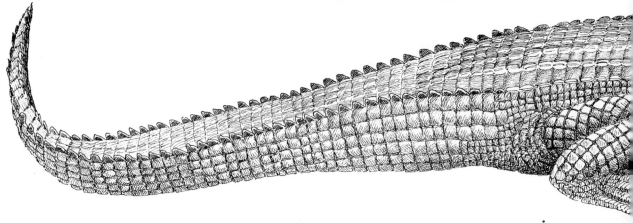

(4.5 meters) long. They had long, slim jaws, studded with sharp teeth. Their nostrils were on a little bump, high up on their heads. When a phytosaur swam, only the bump showed above the water. This enabled a phytosaur to sneak up on unsuspecting animals that came close to the water's edge.

When phytosaurs were living, there were also some small, short-nosed reptiles about thirty inches (75 centimeters) long. In time, something caused all the phytosaurs to die out. When this happened, the descendants of the little reptiles took over the lakes and streams. And these reptiles slowly became just like phytosaurs—they looked like them and lived like them. They were the first crocodiles. And so, the crocodiles and alligators of today are still "imitating" the phytosaurs whose place they took.

The first crocodiles appeared some 180 million years ago. During the rest of the Age of Reptiles, crocodiles shared the waters of the streams and swamps with the dinosaurs. Near the end of the Age of Reptiles, some crocodiles were as much as fifty feet (15 meters) long, and probably sometimes ate young dinosaurs!

Archaeopteryx

Birds the dinosaurs knew

The Age of Reptiles might very well be called the "birthday" of birds. Why? Because it was during the Age of Reptiles that the first birds appeared.

Birds are descended from reptiles—probably from small reptiles that were closely related to the first kinds of dinosaurs. Over millions of years, the bodies of these little reptiles changed. The scales, especially on their front legs and tails, grew longer—and became feathers. And these little reptiles became warm-blooded and quick moving. They probably scurried about after insects, and in time were able to make long, gliding leaps by spreading out their feathery front legs. These animals were the ancestors of all birds.

The oldest bird we know of is called *Archaeopteryx* (ahr kee AHP tuhr ihks), meaning "ancient-wing." This bird was about the size of a pigeon. It did not have a bill, as birds do now—its head was like a reptile's head, with tiny teeth in the jaws. Although it had wings with long feathers, it also had little claws on its wings. And

it had a long, lizardlike tail, with feathers growing out
of it. *Archaeopteryx* lived about 140 million years
ago, at the same time as such dinosaurs as *Stegosaurus*
and *Allosaurus*.

By about eighty million years ago, a great many new
kinds of birds had appeared. They were much more
like the birds of today than was *Archaeopteryx*. They
had bills and short tails. Most of these birds were good
flyers. But some, like the penguins of today, were
swimmers. And some were runners, like ostriches are.

(continued on page 174)

(continued from page 173)

One of the swimming birds lived on the shore of the same great sea where the giant turtle *Archelon* swam, and where the big winged reptile *Pteranodon* caught fish. This bird, *Hesperornis* (hehs puh RAWR nihs), or "western bird," had only tiny wings and could not fly. But it was a skillful swimmer and diver that lived on fish. It was about five feet (1.5 meters) long. Unlike birds of today, *Hesperornis* had teeth.

For hundreds of years, people have thought of birds and reptiles as two different things. But now, many scientists feel that birds are really part of the reptile group, along with snakes, lizards, turtles, crocodiles, and alligators!

Hesperornis

"Beak-lizards," lizards, and snakes

About two hundred million years ago, creatures called rhynchosaurs (RIHNG koh sawrs) appeared. The name means "beak-lizard." These "beak-lizards" were four-footed reptiles with snouts like beaks. There were many kinds of them during the Age of Reptiles, but they became extinct early on. Some of the "beak-lizards" of long ago were as much as six feet (1.8 meters) in length.

Lizards, too, first appeared about two hundred million years ago. Lizards then, like all the lizards today, were long-tailed, four-footed reptiles.

Snakes are the "newest" reptiles. They first appeared about one hundred million years ago. Their ancestors were lizards that slowly got rid of their legs during millions of years. So snakes are really part of the lizard group of reptiles.

A prehistoric "beak-lizard" (top) and a modern "lizard," the tuatara.

skull of a prehistoric beak-lizard

skull of a tuatara

Two fossil ammonite shells (above). Ammonites were octopuslike creatures with coiled shells. They lived in the sea during the Age of Reptiles.

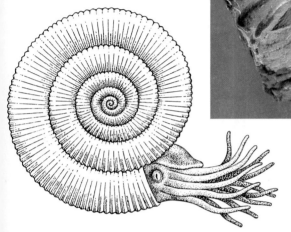

The ocean in the Age of Reptiles

The Age of Reptiles lasted for 210 million years. During all this time there were many changes in the animals that lived in the sea. Old groups of creatures died out. New creatures appeared.

Many kinds of creatures called ammonites (AM uh nyts), a name that means "coiled horn," lived in the sea during the Age of Reptiles. An ammonite was somewhat like an octopus, but its body was covered by a coiled shell. One kind of ammonite was a giant. Its shell was about six feet (1.8 meters) wide! But by the time the Age of Reptiles ended, all the ammonites had become extinct.

There were giant fishes, too, during the Age of Reptiles. One was fifteen feet (4.5 meters) long. A fossil skeleton of this giant fish was found with the skeleton of a fish the size of a man in its stomach!

Early in the Age of Reptiles, the last of the trilobites, which had lived in the seas for hundreds of millions of years, became extinct. And most of the brachiopods, the clamlike animals that had shared the ocean with the trilobites for all those years, were gone, too. Only a few kinds survived.

But a great many of the kinds of animals that live in the ocean today first appeared during the Age of Reptiles. For it was at that time that oysters, lobsters, octopuses, squids, crabs, many kinds of corals, and modern fish and modern sharks came into the world.

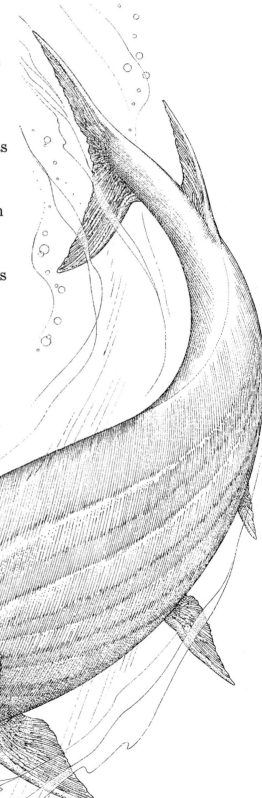

A giant fish of eighty million years ago.

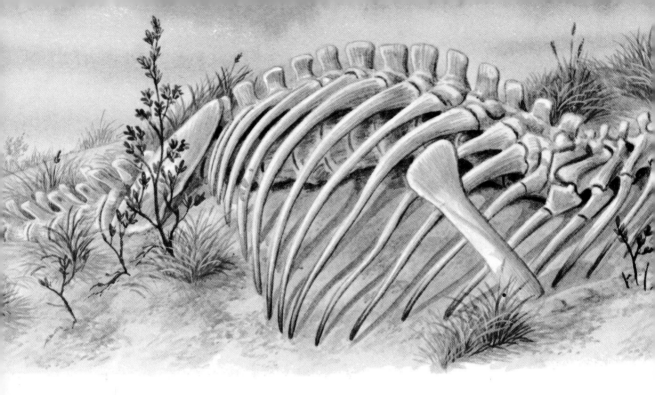

The end of the Age of Reptiles

Many kinds of animals now living in the world are in danger of becoming extinct. This means that they are slowly becoming fewer and fewer, and someday will be gone—forever.

This is what happened to many of the creatures that lived during the Age of Reptiles. Between seventy million and sixty-five million years ago, the dinosaurs, many other kinds of reptiles, and some of the animals that lived in the sea became extinct. They all died out and are now gone from the earth.

This did not take place all at once. It probably took millions of years. Slowly, during all that time, the dinosaurs and many other creatures became fewer and fewer—just as is happening to some kinds of animals right now.

But today, animals are becoming fewer and fewer, mainly because of the activities of people. Animals

are being crowded out by cities, roads, and farms.
They are being poisoned by pollution caused by cars,
airplanes, ships, and factories. But there were none
of these things during the Age of Reptiles. So why
did dinosaurs and other animals become extinct?

There were probably many causes. The world was
changing during the last part of the Age of Reptiles.
New kinds of plants were taking the place of old
ones. Mountains were pushing up where seas had
once covered the land. New kinds of animals, such as
birds, may have been crowding out old ones, such as
the flying reptiles. There may have been climate
changes or maybe a huge meteorite struck the earth.

Perhaps all these things, and others that we don't
know about, caused the dinosaurs to die off. We
really don't know for sure. It's a kind of mystery.

But when the dinosaurs and other kinds of reptiles
disappeared forever, it was the end of the Age of
Reptiles. A new age—the Age of Mammals—began.

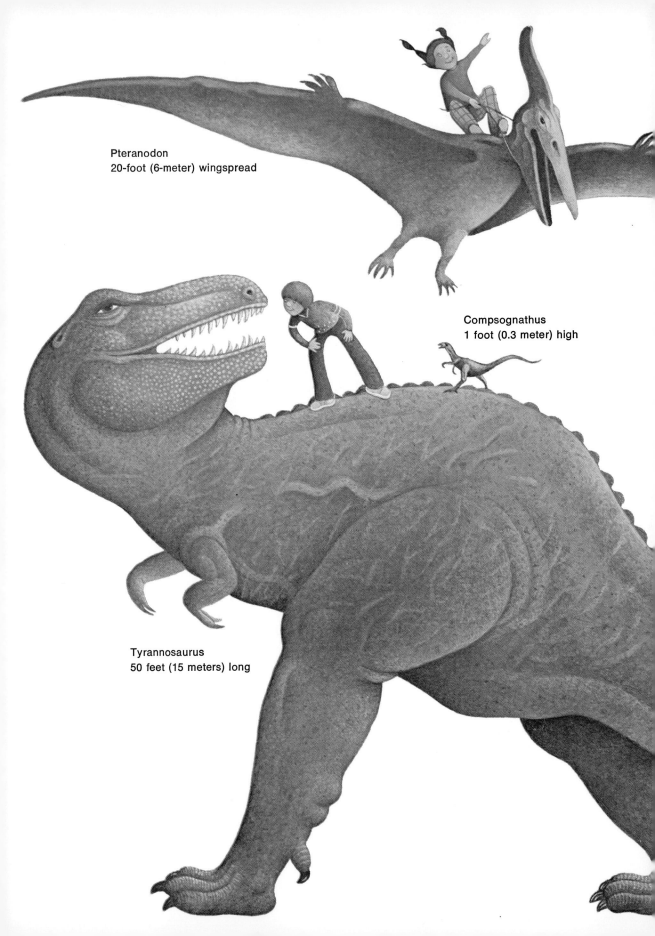

Pteranodon
20-foot (6-meter) wingspread

Compsognathus
1 foot (0.3 meter) high

Tyrannosaurus
50 feet (15 meters) long

Elasmosaurus (a plesiosaur)
44 feet (13.2 meters) long

How big were they?

Some dinosaurs, such as *Tyrannosaurus*, were giants. Others, like *Monoclonius*, were medium-sized. And some, such as *Compsognathus*, were small. *Pteranodon* was a large flying reptile. *Elasmosaurus* was one of the largest sea reptiles.

Monoclonius
17 feet (5.1 meters) long

How big were they?

The long-necked, plant-eating dinosaurs were the biggest animals that have ever lived on land. And the biggest of all was *Brachiosaurus*. Its head was forty feet (12 meters) above the ground!

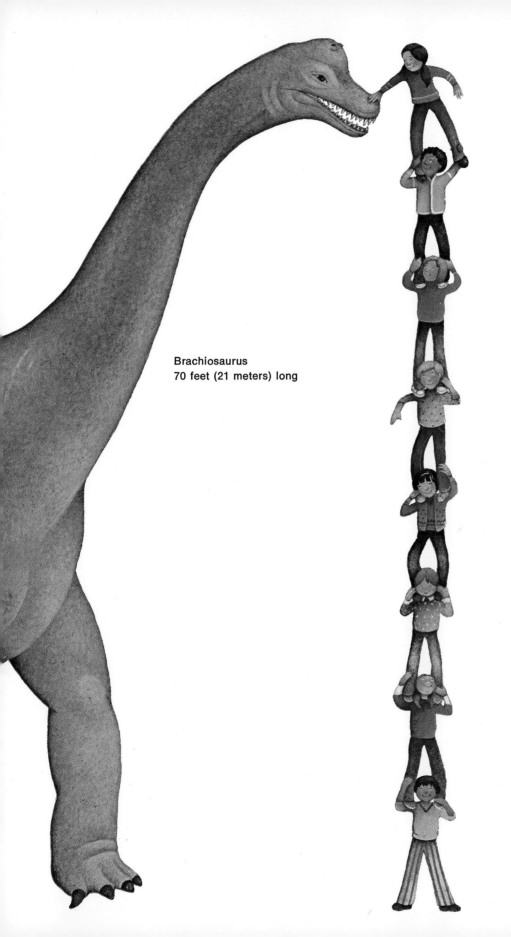

Brachiosaurus
70 feet (21 meters) long

184

Coelophysis
200 million
years ago

Apatosaurus
150 million years ago

Iguanodon
125 million years ago

When did they live?

Between two hundred million and seventy million years ago, the reptiles called dinosaurs ruled the earth. Early dinosaurs, such as *Coelophysis*, were small, two-legged, meat-eaters. Later, there were big, two-legged, plant-eaters, such as *Iguanodon*, and four-footed ones, such as *Triceratops* and the huge *Apatosaurus*. And there were giant meat-eaters, such as *Tyrannosaurus*.

**Tyrannosaurus
70 million years ago**

**Triceratops
70 million years ago**

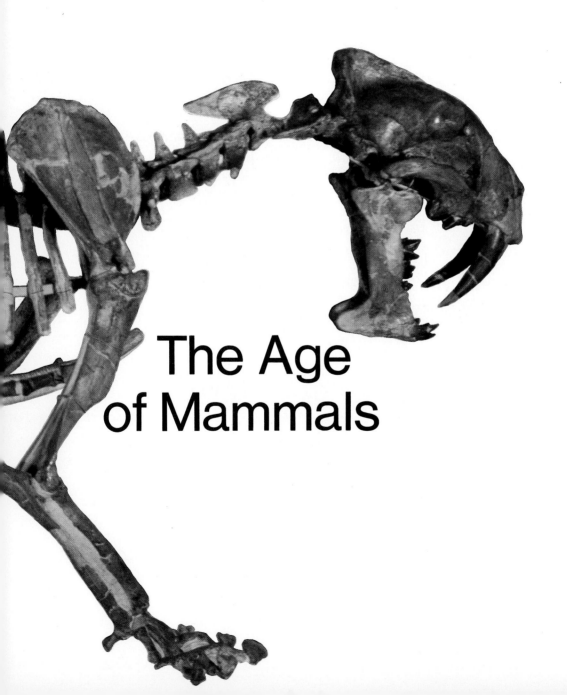

The Age
of Mammals

By the end of the Age of Reptiles, the world was much like it is now. A variety of plants covered the plains and there were now many kinds of flowers. Oaks, willows, and other trees of today grew in thick forests. But mixed in with them were palm trees and other tropical plants, for the world was still warm all year round.

Gone were the dinosaurs and most of the other reptiles that had owned the world for millions of years. Of course, there were many kinds of insects and birds. There were also small, furry creatures about the size of a rat—the kind of animal that is called a mammal.

In the Age of Reptiles these mammals were small and stayed hidden. But now they were spreading out into the world. And they were changing. Some of them were getting bigger. Many of them were taking on new ways of life and new shapes.

The mammals were taking the place of the reptiles as masters of the world. By sixty-five million years ago, a new age was beginning—the Age of Mammals. This is the age *we* are living in now.

on the next page ▶
By about sixty million years ago, furry, warm-blooded mammals, such as *Barylambda,* were the rulers of the earth.

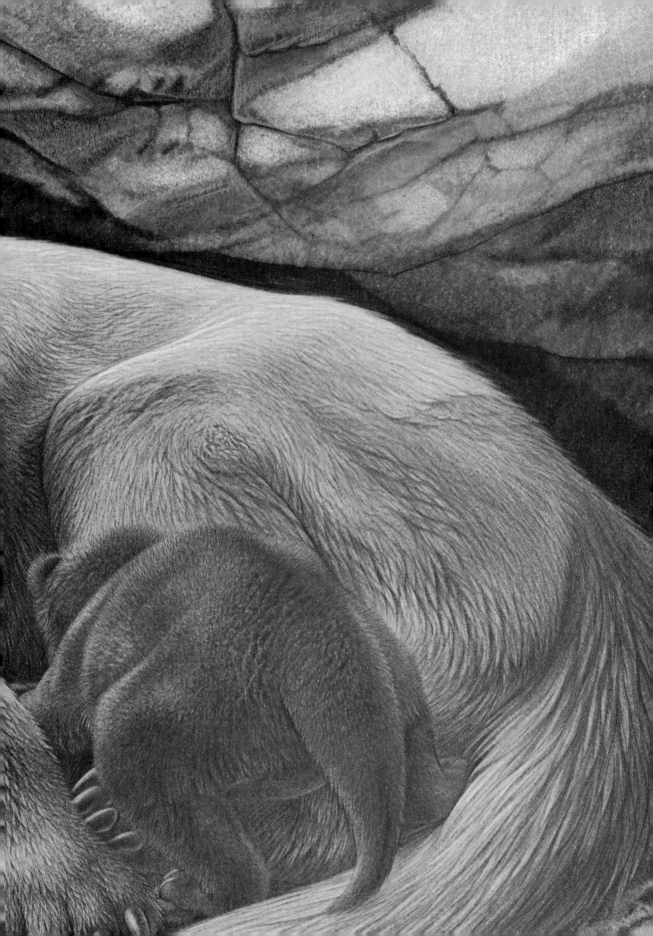

Look Alikes
The modern shrew (above) is much like a mammal (below) of 135 million years ago.

The new animals

About 180 million years ago, animals of a new kind appeared in the world. They were probably descended from one kind of reptile that had slowly changed during millions of years.

These changed reptiles had a somewhat different kind of skeleton. They were also warm-blooded animals, not cold-blooded as are most reptiles. They had hairy skin instead of scales. And the bodies of the mothers were able to make milk for the babies to drink.

These new creatures were the kind of animal we call a mammal. Cows, horses, cats, dogs, dolphins, whales, mice, bats, monkeys, and humans are some of the many kinds of mammals living today.

The first mammals probably laid eggs, as did their reptile ancestors. Even now, there are mammals that lay eggs. They are the platypus and the spiny anteater of Australia. These two egg-laying mammals are like reptiles in many ways. But like all mammals, they are warm-blooded, hairy, and feed their babies milk. They show us what some of the first mammals may have been like.

By about 135 million years ago, almost all mammals probably had babies instead of laying eggs. One kind of mammal living then was a little creature about the size of a rat or a mouse. It had a mouselike body

opossum

The platypus of today is probably much like the first egg-laying mammals. The modern opossum, a marsupial, or pouched mammal, is much like the first marsupials.

platypus

and a pointed nose. It looked very much like the tiny animals called shrews that are common now. Little creatures like these were probably the ancestors of most of the mammals of today.

By around eighty million years ago, there were the two main groups of mammals there are now. We call one group placental mammals. These mammals have babies that are soon able to see and walk—as are kittens and puppies. The other group have babies that are not fully formed when they are born. So the babies are kept in a pouch on the mother's stomach until they are able to care for themselves. A mammal that carries its babies in a pouch—like a kangaroo—is called a marsupial. The first kind of marsupials looked much like the opossum of today.

When the Age of Reptiles ended, mammals quickly spread out into the world. They began to change in shape and size and to take on new ways of life.

The first big mammals

The mammals that began to take over the world at the end of the Age of Reptiles were all quite small. But in time, some of the plant-eating mammals became rather large.

One of the first of the really big mammals is called *Uintatherium* (yoo ihn tuh THIHR ee uhm), or "beast of the Uinta." Its fossil skeletons are found near the Uinta Mountains of Utah. *Uintatherium* was about as big as a rhinoceros—twelve feet (3.6 meters) long and seven feet (2.1 meters) high.

Uintatherium was a heavy, bulky beast with great, thick legs and a big head. It had three pair of thick, knobby horns on its head. The male had a long, pointed tooth sticking down from each side of the mouth. *Uintatherium* was probably able to defend itself against meat-eating mammals.

Uintatherium

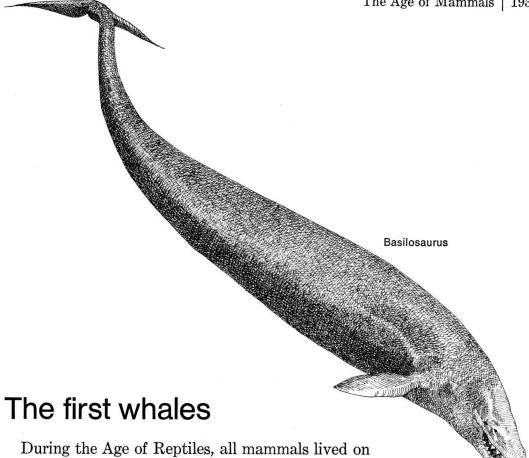

Basilosaurus

The first whales

During the Age of Reptiles, all mammals lived on land. The sea was a dangerous place for them because of the many huge reptiles living there. But as the reptiles began to die out, some mammals took to the water. Slowly, during millions of years, they became sea creatures. Some became the first kinds of whales.

The oldest whales we know anything about lived fifty million years ago. They are called zeuglodonts (ZOO gluh dahnts), or "loop tooth," because of the way their teeth are formed. The largest zeuglodont was a huge creature more than sixty feet (18 meters) long. It was longer and slimmer than the whales of today, with a smaller head. And its mouth was full of sharp teeth. It must have looked more like a sea serpent than a whale! That is why this whale is called a *Basilosaurus* (bas uh luh SAWR uhs), or "king lizard."

The first meat-eating mammals

A small mammal dug busily among the roots of a tree. It did not see, hear, or smell the slightly larger, doglike creature that was creeping toward it. The doglike creature crouched down, its muscles tense. Then, showing its sharp teeth, it leaped!

The mammals that lived during the Age of Reptiles probably ate anything they could get—leaves, fruit, insects, the flesh of dead creatures they found, or the flesh of smaller animals they managed to kill. But by the time the Age of Mammals began, some mammals had become skilled hunters that ate only the flesh of animals they killed.

The first of the meat-eating mammals in the Age of Mammals are called creodonts (KREE uh dahnts). The

name means "flesh-tooth." At first, these animals
were small, about the size of a rat. Later, by about
fifty million years ago, they were the size of a large
dog. They even looked somewhat like dogs and cats.
But they were not the ancestors of any animal living
today. After a time, they all died out.

The actual ancestors of dogs, cats, and all the other
meat-eating animals of today were little creatures,
about the size of a squirrel. They are called miacids
(MY uh sihdz), a name that means "small pointed."
The creatures were given this name because of the
shape of their teeth.

Miacids looked much like the weasels of today. They
probably lived in forests and may have been tree
dwellers. They may have caught their prey by leaping
from the branches of trees.

The world of the mammals

Clear, fast-moving streams flow down from the high mountains. Where the land is low, the streams come together to form a swamp. A thick forest of trees grows in this swampy area. There are leafy oaks and elms, as well as tall palms with slim, straight trunks. Bushes and shrubs, many of them bright with flowers, dot the ground.

The air in the forest is warm and heavy and damp. Insects chitter, buzz, and whir. The cry of a bird rings out. A long, black-and-brown snake slips down out of the branches of a tree and slowly zigzags away. Alligators doze among the bulrushes at the edge of the swamp.

Half a dozen small animals are browsing upon some leafy bushes. The little animals glance nervously about as they munch their meal of leaves. They must always be alert. They have many enemies. These plant-eaters are slim, dainty creatures, about the size of a small dog. Their bodies are rather doglike, with long, pointed tails. But their heads are somewhat like a deer's head. They have spread-out toes rather than hoofs, but they are horses—the first horses. For this is *Eohippus* (ee oh HIHP uhs), the "dawn horse."

A short distance away, from a shadowy spot among some thick bushes, an enemy watches! It is patiently waiting for the little horses to move a bit nearer. It is an *Oxyaena* (ahk see EE nuh), a flesh-eater. About the size of a large dog, it has a blunt, catlike head and a long, pointed tail. And it, too, has spread-out toes.

From the nearby swamp comes the sound of snorts and splashes. Several large *Coryphodon*s (kuh RIHF uh dahns) are wading around in the water. They are about the size of a cow, with bulky bodies, short legs, and big heads. Sharp tusks stick out of the corners of their

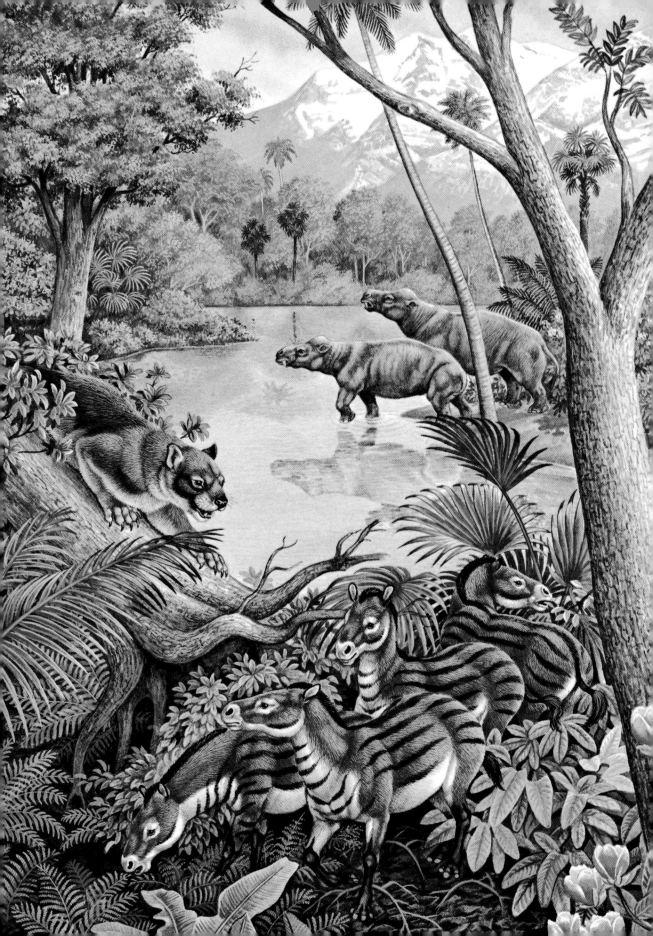

(continued from page 196)

mouths. In fact, their name means "sharp tooth." But these animals are not meat-eaters—they use their tusks to defend themselves.

The sun is setting and the forest grows dark. Tiny lights wink among the trees as fireflies rise into the air. Small, winged shapes dart and swoop here and there. The bats, mammals with wings, have awakened from their day's sleep and are out hunting for insects.

From a tree branch, a little animal peers down at a hungry alligator crawling through the underbrush toward the water. The animal looks somewhat like a monkey with the head of a fox. It is a *Notharctus* (nuh THAHRK tuhs). In spite of its name, which means "false bear," this animal is an ancestor of monkeys.

The time when all these creatures lived was about fifty-five million to forty-five million years ago. That was long after the Age of Reptiles had come to an end. The little mammals that had lived among the dinosaurs had changed into many different kinds of creatures.

During millions of years, some of their descendants changed even more. For some of the mammals that lived in that swampy forest millions of years ago were the ancestors of animals that are common today.

Arsinoitherium

Mystery mammals

About forty million years ago there was a mammal with a body somewhat like that of an elephant and a head somewhat like that of a rhinoceros. Two huge horns that stuck up side by side covered most of its forehead and snout. This creature was about the size of a rhinoceros. It is named *Arsinoitherium* (ahr sih noy THIHR ee uhm), which means something like "dangerous beast."

Scientists have found both the ancestors and the descendants of most prehistoric mammals. But they haven't been able to find *Arsinoitherium*'s ancestors or descendants. So *Arsinoitherium* is a mystery—an animal that doesn't seem to be related to any of the mammals of today or of prehistoric times.

Twenty-five million years ago, there was an animal that looked somewhat like a horse. We expect animals like horses to have hoofs. But this animal had thick, clumsy legs and claws on all of its toes. When scientists first found the bones of this creature, they thought its head and body belonged to one kind of animal and its legs and feet to another.

This animal was named *Moropus* (MAWR uh puhs), meaning "foolish-footed." What could it have used its strange, clawed feet for? Did it stand up on its back legs and use its front claws to pull down branches of trees so it could eat the leaves? We just don't know. Like *Arsinoitherium*, *Moropus* is a mystery.

Moropus

Fearsome birds

There were some very fearsome birds living long ago. These birds were quite large, and ran on the ground instead of flying. And they were fierce hunters.

One of these kinds of birds lived in North America about fifty million years ago. It was seven feet (2.1 meters) tall. Its head was nearly as big as that of a horse, with a sharp, curved beak. It could not fly, for its wings were much too tiny to lift its big body off the ground. But judging by its sturdy, powerful legs, it must have been a good runner. It probably often

Phororhacos

hunted small mammals, such as the little dog-sized horses that lived then.

This big bird's name is *Diatryma* (dy uh TRY muh). The name means "through a hole," and describes the way the bird's foot bones are formed.

About twenty-five million years ago, a bird much like *Diatryma* lived in South America. About five feet (1.5 meters) tall, it was not quite as big and bulky as *Diatryma*. But it was probably a faster runner. It lived on open plains and may have hunted other birds, small mammals, and reptiles.

This bird's name is *Phororhacos* (foh RAWR uh kuhs), meaning "ragged thief." Perhaps the scientist who named it thought it had rather shaggy feathers and was as quick as a thief.

The idea of a bird that cannot fly may seem strange. But even today there are birds—ostriches, penguins, and several others—that can't fly.

Eohippus

The story of the horse

The story of the horse begins some fifty-five million years ago, not very long after the beginning of the Age of Mammals.

At that time, in the western part of North America and in Europe, there lived some little animals about the size of a fox terrier. They were slender and graceful animals. They had little feet with spread-out toes—four toes on each front foot and three on each back foot. And there was a little hoof on each toe. These dainty little creatures were forest animals. They moved from place to place in the forest, eating soft leaves and fruit.

They were the first horses, the ancestors of all the horses in the world now. The proper name for this animal is *Hyracotherium* (hy ruh koh THIHR ee uhm). But many scientists like to call it *Eohippus* (ee oh HIHP uhs), or "dawn horse." This is a good name, because these animals lived at the earliest part, or "dawn," of the Age of Mammals.

Something went wrong for the descendants of the little European horses. They all died out, and no horses were left anywhere but in North America. But the descendants of the American *Eohippus* did very well. And, as millions of years went by, they changed.

By about thirty-five million years ago, some of *Eohippus'* descendants were the size of a large dog, such as a collie. They now had three toes on all four of their feet. The middle toe on each foot was bigger than the other toes, with a bigger hoof. This horse is called *Mesohippus* (mehs oh HIHP uhs), or "middle horse." And in appearance it was just about midway between little *Eohippus* and the horses of today.

It was during the time of *Mesohippus* that horses started to eat grass. This was a time when the world

Mesohippus

(continued from page 205)

was changing. Swamps and forests were giving way to grassy plains. There was less and less food for those horses that could chew only soft leaves and fruits. But some horses had teeth that could chew the tough grass. So these animals had plenty of food. While the other horses slowly died out, the grass-eaters survived. And they had babies that could eat grass, too. Finally, only the grass-eating horses were left.

There was another change about this time. Once again, as had happened before, the continents of North America and Asia were connected by a broad strip of land. Many horses moved across this "bridge" from Alaska into Asia. From there, they spread out into Europe and Africa. Later, horses from North America moved down into South America.

About twenty-five million years ago, a horse we call *Merychippus* (mehr ih KIHP uhs) was living on the plains. *Merychippus* means "grass-eating horse," and all horses were now grass-eaters. *Merychippus* was about the size of a sheep and looked much like horses do now. It still had three toes on each foot, but the two outside toes had become tiny, while the middle toe had become larger and longer. Thus *Merychippus* was actually walking on only one toe, just like the horses of today.

As millions of years went by, horses grew bigger. At the same time, their middle toes grew bigger and longer. The two little toes slowly disappeared. Finally, about a million years ago, the kind of horse that lives today came into the world—an animal that had only one toe covered with a large hoof.

Then, about twenty-five thousand years ago, just as had once happened in Europe, all the horses in North and South America died out. There were no more horses in the Western Hemisphere until 1519, nearly five hundred years ago. That was when the Spanish explorer Hernando Cortes brought horses with him to Mexico. So all the horses in the Americas are descended from horses that came from Europe. But *those* horses were descended from horses that had come from North America in the first place!

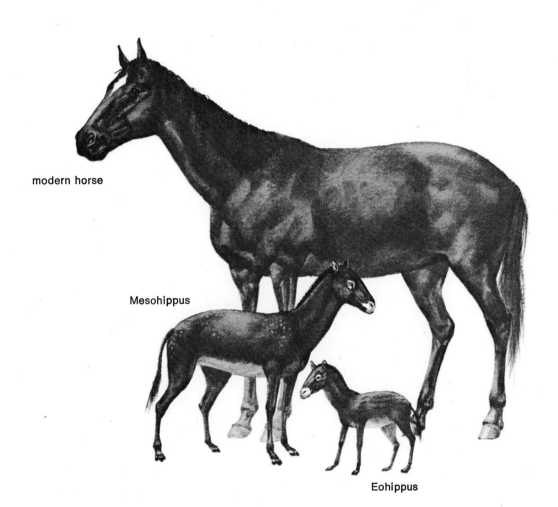

modern horse

Mesohippus

Eohippus

The "giant beasts"

Eohippus, the little horse of fifty-five million years ago, shared the forests it lived in with many other kinds of creatures. One of these was an animal that looked rather like *Eohippus*. It was about the same size and shape, but had a bulkier body and thicker legs. It looked a bit like a small, plump horse.

This little creature was one of the first of the great animals called titanotheres (ty TAN uh thihrs), or "giant beasts." That seems like a strange name for such a little animal—but some of its descendants were indeed giants.

Forty million years ago, there was a titanothere that

Brontotherium

has been named *Brontotherium* (brahn tuh THIHR ee uhm), meaning "thunder beast." It was a huge, lumbering creature, about eight feet (2.4 meters) high and fifteen feet (4.5 meters) long. It looked somewhat like a rhinoceros, but was much bigger and heavier. And instead of having a pointed horn on its nose, as rhinos do, *Brontotherium* had a thick, Y-shaped horn. It probably used this horn when fighting with others of its kind.

Brontotherium and several other kinds of these big titanotheres lived on plains in the western part of North America, and in Asia, for millions of years. All the titanotheres became extinct about thirty-five million years ago.

Apes of long ago

The sun was rising. It sparkled on the water of a broad river. It gleamed on the leaves of the trees along the river's banks. Slowly, the forest around the river began to awaken. Bird calls sounded among the trees. Grunts and splashes came from the river, where some animals were beginning their morning feeding. A huge, bulky beast with two enormous horns on its head plodded to the river's edge. Lowering its head, the beast drank with noisy gulps.

In the trees, some creatures that had been sleeping among the branches awakened. Rather monkeylike animals, they had tails and long snouts. They were about the size of a very small child. Chattering noisily, they began to move around among the branches in search of food.

This forest grew where the land of Egypt is now. The monkeylike creatures lived there about forty million years ago. They are named *Aegyptopithecus* (ee jihp tuh PITH uh kuhs), which means "Egypt ape." Actually, they were not really apes. For one thing, apes do not have a tail. But scientists think that the "Egypt apes" were probably the ancestors of the chimpanzees, gorillas, and other apes of today.

Forty million years ago, Africa, Europe, and Asia were all more closely connected than they are now. During millions of years, the animals that were the descendants of *Aegyptopithecus* spread through all these lands.

Fifteen to twenty million years ago, creatures that were probably descendants of *Aegyptopithecus* lived in Europe, Africa, and Asia. These creatures are called *Dryopithecus* (dry uh PITH uh kuhs), or "oak ape."

(continued on page 212)

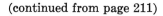

(continued from page 211)

They were given this name because prints of oak leaves were found in the rocks in which the first *Dryopithecus* fossils were discovered. *Dryopithecus* probably looked and lived much as chimpanzees do today. It probably no longer had a tail. In its search for food—tender buds, fruit, seeds, and insects—it may have spent a lot of time on the ground rather than in trees.

About fifteen million years ago, there was another creature that was probably descended from *Aegyptopithecus*. It was living in southern Asia and Africa. It has been named *Ramapithecus* (ram uh PITH uh kuhs), or "Rama ape," after Rama, a Hindu god.

Scientists think that *Ramapithecus* may have been rather special. For one thing, an ape walks on all fours, using its hands as feet. But *Ramapithecus* may have walked on two legs, as humans do. Also, its teeth resemble human teeth more than do the teeth of most other apes. Scientists think that *Ramapithecus* was an ape that was probably changing into something new. It may have been the ancestor of the creatures that are called—humans!

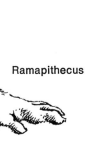

Ramapithecus

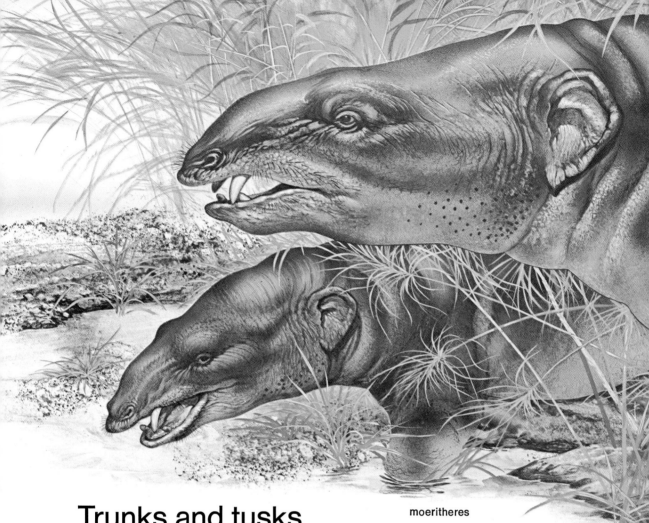

moeritheres

Trunks and tusks

Forty million years ago, pudgy animals about as high as a man's knee lived along lakes and rivers in Africa. These animals probably spent much of their time in the warm water, swimming and wading about in search of juicy plants to eat. They had short, thick legs and rather long noses. Pairs of large, sharp teeth stuck out of their upper and lower jaws.

Scientists named the creatures moeritheres (MIHR uh thihrz). The name means "beast of Lake Moeris," the name of an ancient lake near where these animals lived. The little moeritheres were the ancestors of the biggest land animals in the world today—the great family of elephants!

(continued on page 214)

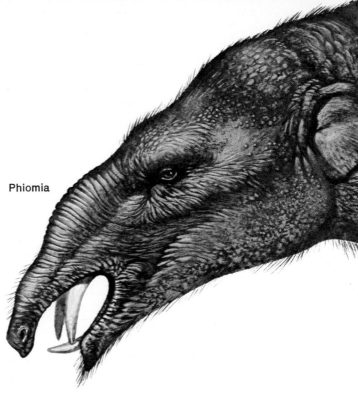

Phiomia

(continued from page 213)

As a few million years went by, the moeritheres changed, a little at a time. One way they changed was to get bigger—until they were about as high as a man. The two pair of teeth that stuck out of their mouths grew longer and became tusks. Their noses grew and became trunks. They were now a new kind of animal that looked a little more like an elephant.

This creature has been named *Phiomia* (fy OH mee uh). During a few million more years, descendants of *Phiomia* moved into North America, Europe, and Asia. They were the animals we call mastodons (MAS tuh dahns), a name that refers to the shape of their teeth. These animals were much like the elephants of today, but they were larger and huskier.

By about twenty-five million years ago, some other descendants of the moeritheres had become animals that are called deinotheres (DY nuh thihrz), meaning "terrible beasts." Deinotheres looked very much like elephants except for their tusks. An elephant's tusks

Platybelodon

mastodons

(continued from page 215)

Another animal descended from moeritheres was
Platybelodon (plat ee BEHL uh dahn). This prehistoric
creature lived in Asia about twenty million years ago.
The name *Platybelodon* means "flat front tooth." The
animal was given this name because its two lower
tusks were broad and flat. These tusks, which were in
the lower jaw, formed a sort of huge shovel! The
animal probably used this "shovel" to scoop up water
plants from shallow lakes and streams.

Other descendants of moeritheres appeared about
four million years ago. They were the kind of elephant
we call a mammoth (MAM uhth). It is a good name,
for mammoth means "big." And these animals were
enormous, shaggy creatures with great curling tusks.

Until about ten thousand years ago, there were a
great many big animals with trunks and tusks in most
parts of the world. Now, only two kinds of elephants
are left. One lives in Africa and the other in Asia.

stick out from the upper jaw and curve up. But the deinotheres' tusks were in the lower jaw and curved downward, like huge hooks. Scientists think that the deinotheres may have used their great tusks to dig for roots. The biggest deinotheres were about ten feet (3 meters) high.

(continued on page 216)

deinotherium

The nose-horns

Next to the elephant, the rhinoceros is the biggest
of all land animals. It is a great, heavy, lumbering
beast with one or two horns on its nose. In fact, the
name rhinoceros means "nose-horn."

But the first kind of rhinoceroses had no horn. They
weren't a bit like the rhinos of today. They were little
animals, only about as big as a large dog, such as a St.
Bernard. Scientists call them "running rhinoceroses"
because they were probably very fast runners. They
lived in the forests of North America, about forty-five
million years ago.

A few million years later there were some bigger
rhinos. But they still weren't much like the rhinos of
today. They were more like hippopotamuses! They

had thick bodies and very short legs. Some had horns and some did not. Most of these animals were quite large, as much as fourteen feet (4.2 meters) long. They probably spent most of their time splashing about in lakes and rivers.

As time went on, many different kinds of rhinos appeared. Some of them still had no horns. Others had a small, knobby sort of horn. And some had two horns that were side by side on their noses.

(continued on page 220)

Look Alikes

The hippopotamus (right), which spends much of its time in lakes and streams, resembles a prehistoric rhinoceros called *Teleoceras* (tehl ee AHS uhr uhs). *Teleoceras* (above) lived about twelve million years ago. It, too, probably spent much of its time in water.

Baluchitherium

(continued from page 219)

One of the hornless rhinoceroses was the biggest mammal that has ever lived on the land—much bigger than any elephant. It was eighteen feet (5.4 meters) high and thirty-four feet (10.2 meters) long. That's as big as many dinosaurs were!

These giant rhinos lived about twenty million years ago, in a part of Asia that is called Baluchistan. They were named *Baluchitherium* (buh loo chuh THIHR ee uhm), meaning "the beast of Baluchistan." Their heads were rather small for their huge bodies, but were still more than four feet (1.2 meters) long!

All the rhinoceroses in North America died out by about ten million years ago. However, there were still rhinos in Africa, Asia, and Europe. During the Ice Age, rhinoceroses in Europe and northern Asia were covered with thick, woolly coats of fur.

But, by about ten thousand years ago, all the rhinos had died out except for five kinds—three kinds in Asia and two kinds in Africa. And these rhinos, too, appear to be dying out. Some of them may become extinct even during your lifetime.

The fossil skull of a prehistoric rhinoceros.

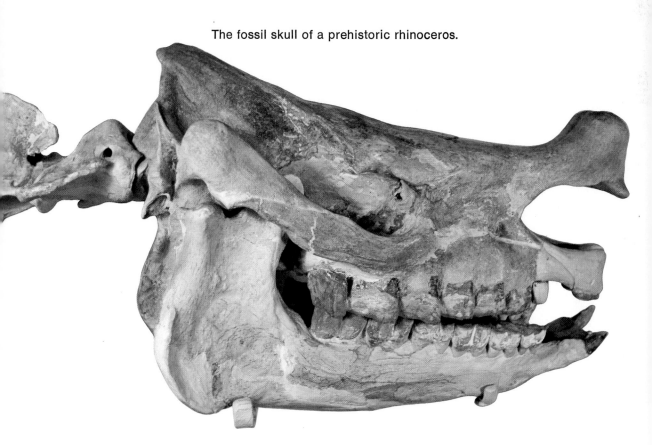

All kinds of camels

Think of a camel and you'll probably think of a desert. For, as everyone knows, camels live in the great, hot, sandy deserts of North Africa and Asia.

But the camel wasn't always a desert animal. And it didn't always live in Africa or Asia. As a matter of fact, camels began in North America! More than forty million years before there were camels anywhere else, there were camels where Canada, the United States, and Mexico are now!

The ancestors of today's camels were small creatures, only about the size of a cat. They probably lived in forests and ate leaves and fruit. In time, they moved out of the forests and onto the plains. Slowly, they got bigger.

By thirty-five million years ago, some of these members of the camel family were about the size of a sheep. They had much shorter necks and legs than the camels of today. And they probably did not have humps. These creatures probably lived in herds, like horses.

About fifteen million years ago, several kinds of camels roamed over the plains of North America. One kind was a slim little animal about the size of a large dog. This was *Stenomylus* (stehn uh MY luhs). It is often called the "gazelle camel." It could probably run as fast as a gazelle, which is one of the fastest animals today.

(continued on page 225)

A fossil skeleton of *Stenomylus,* often called the "gazelle camel."

Stenomylus

Procamelus

Procamelus, or "first camel,"
lived in North America about
fifteen million years ago. Both
the dromedary of Africa and Asia
and the guanaco of South America
are descended from *Procamelus.*

guanaco

dromedary

(continued from page 222)

At the same time as the "gazelle camels," there were also "giraffe camels." They had long, skinny legs and very long necks. Their heads were some twelve to fourteen feet (4.2 to 5.4 meters) above the ground. They probably ate leaves, fruits, and twigs from trees. Their name is *Aepycamelus* (eh pi kuh MEE luhs), which means "high camel."

There was also a small camel called *Procamelus* (proh kuh MEE luhs), living about fifteen million years ago. *Procamelus* means "first camel," and this animal was the ancestor of the camels of today.

For a time, as had happened before, North America was connected to Asia and to South America. During this period, descendants of *Procamelus* moved into both these lands.

Some of the camels that moved into Asia went on to Africa. Slowly, they became desert animals, as they are today. Others moved into South America. They became the animals we know as llamas and guanacos. Llamas haven't changed much. They still look very much like the kinds of camels that traveled to South America millions of years ago.

So, at one time, there were camels of different kinds in North America, South America, Asia, and Africa. But then, something happened. All of the camels in North America died out. No one knows why. But in North America, where camels began and where they lived for millions of years, not one was left.

Mammals with pouches

Mammals that carry their babies in a pouch are called marsupials. The best-known marsupial in the world today is the kangaroo of Australia. But in prehistoric times there were marsupials, too.

In Australia, about fifty thousand years ago, there was one kind of kangaroo that stood nearly nine feet (2.7 meters) high. That's about two feet higher than the tallest kangaroo today. Its front legs were longer than those of a modern kangaroo, and its nose was shorter. It is often called the "short-faced" kangaroo.

(continued on page 228)

short-faced kangaroo

(continued from page 226)

Another Australian marsupial of fifty thousand years ago was *Diprotodon* (dy PROH tuh dahn). That name means "two front teeth." *Diprotodon* had two big teeth, like curved chisels, at the front of the upper jaw and two small tusks in the lower jaw. It was a big, four-footed animal. A man's head would have reached only a little higher than the highest part of its back.

Both the short-faced kangaroo and *Diprotodon* were plant-eaters. But there were also many meat-eating marsupials in Australia.

Imagine an animal that looks like a lion but carries its baby in a pouch like a kangaroo! No, that isn't a "made-up" animal. There really was such a creature in Australia, long ago. Although it looked very much like a lion, it wasn't a member of the cat family at all. This meat-eating marsupial simply looked like a big cat—a cat that carried its babies in a pouch!

There were also many meat-eating marsupials living in South America in prehistoric times. One kind lived about twenty-five million years ago. It had sharp teeth and probably looked much like a big dog.

Another kind, that lived about fourteen million years ago, was the size of a tiger. It looked very much like a big cat. It had a pair of huge, curved teeth that stuck down from each side of its upper jaw.

Even though one of these animals looked like a dog and the other like a cat, they were not related to dogs or cats. They were marsupials and carried their babies in a pouch.

Most of the marsupials in South America became extinct. They were "squeezed out" by other animals that came down from North America. But this didn't happen in Australia.

Diprotodon

Some two hundred million years ago, all the seven continents we know today were "locked" together like the pieces of a giant jigsaw puzzle. Slowly, this great continent began to break up. In time, Australia became a separate continent. Because it was surrounded by water, few new animals could get there.

So the marsupials were the "owners" of Australia until humans came. To this day, Australia is the home of most of the world's marsupials.

Saber-toothed cats

On a great, grassy plain lies a small, clear, water hole. The water gleams in the light of the bright afternoon sun. Around the water hole, the grass grows in tall, thick clumps.

Crouching in the grass near the water hole is a huge cat. Sticking down out of its mouth are a pair of teeth six inches (15 centimeters) long. The teeth look like sharp daggers.

In the distance there is the sound of crunching grass. Something is coming. The cat lies motionless, close to the ground, hidden by the tall grass. A young ground sloth, the size of a cow, trudges slowly to the water hole. Lowering its head, the sloth begins to drink.

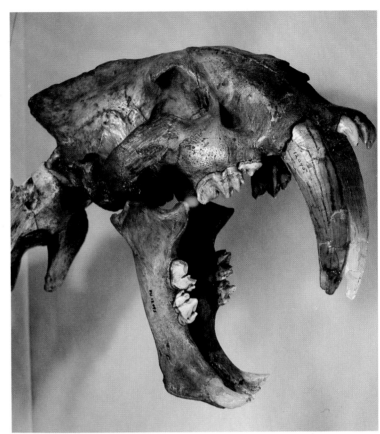

The fossil skull of a *Smilodon*.

Slowly, the big cat slides its body closer and closer.
Suddenly it leaps! In a single bound it crashes down
on the sloth, its mouth open tremendously wide. As it
hits, the cat thrusts its head down, stabbing its two
long teeth into the sloth's neck.

Hunters such as this one lived in many parts of the
world a million years ago. We have given these cats the
name *Smilodon* (SMY luh dahn), a name that means
"carving-knife tooth." However, they are often called
"saber-toothed" cats because their two big teeth were
shaped like a sword called a saber.

The saber-toothed cats were nearly the size of a lion.
But their bodies were stockier and their legs shorter.
These big cats all died out about twenty thousand
years ago.

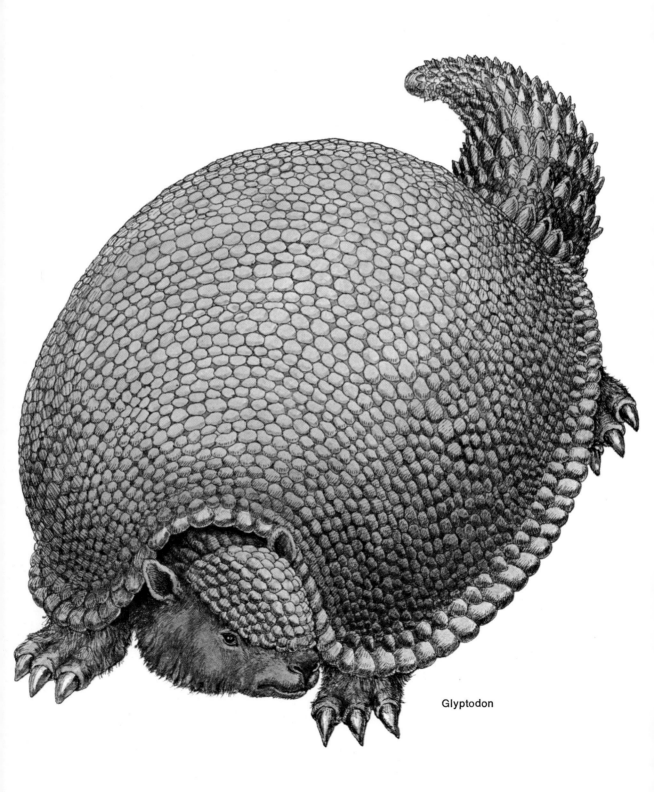

Glyptodon

A mammal in armor

Once upon a time there was a mammal that had a helmet on its head, a shell like a turtle, and a war club for a tail!

No, this is not a fairy tale. There really was such an animal. This strange creature lived a million years ago, in South and Central America and in parts of North America. On its head was a kind of bony cap, like a helmet. Its body was covered by a big, bony shell that was hard as rock. And its thick, heavy tail was covered with knobs and lumps of thick bone. It was a large animal, sometimes as much as nine feet (2.7 meters) long and four feet (1.2 meters) high.

This armored mammal is called *Glyptodon* (GLIHP tuh dahn). The name means "carved tooth." *Glyptodon*'s teeth look as if they had been carefully carved.

Glyptodon lived on plains, among the tall, waving grass. Several kinds of fierce meat-eating animals also lived on those plains. But *Glyptodon* probably had little to fear from them. All it had to do was crouch down and duck its head. Then it became a big dome of rock-hard bone! Even a saber-toothed cat couldn't bite through that tough shell. And if a meat-eater got too close, *Glyptodon* could use its war-club tail. One fast swing of that heavy, bone-covered tail would crack an animal's bones!

But *Glyptodon* was not a fierce creature. It used its armor and tail only to defend itself as it wandered the plains in search of food—probably insects, worms, and some kinds of plants. *Glyptodon*s all died out about twenty-five thousand years ago.

The giant sloth

A huge shaggy animal about the size of an elephant is lumbering across a grassy plain. It looks a little like a great, bulky bear. But this animal has a long, thick tail. It walks awkwardly, on the knuckles of its front feet and the sides of its back ones.

The big beast heads for a clump of trees. When it reaches them, it rears up, standing on its back legs. It reaches its clawed paws into a tree and pulls a branch down toward its head. Its long tongue licks out and pulls a cluster of leaves into its mouth.

Megatherium (mehg uh THIHR ee uhm), or "giant beast," lived in South America and southern North

Megatherium

America about a million years ago. It is the kind of animal called a sloth. There are sloths living in South America today, but they are much smaller and live in trees. *Megatherium* was a giant ground sloth.

The "giant-beast" had yellowish-brown fur. Under the fur, in its skin, was a kind of armor, like pebbles of bone. This "armor" might have helped protect the giant sloth from the saber-toothed cats and other meat-eaters. *Megatherium* could probably also use its sharp claws to defend itself. But it was a slow-moving animal. Young *Megatheriums*, despite their size, may have often fallen prey to saber-tooths.

These big animals all died out, probably only a few hundred years ago.

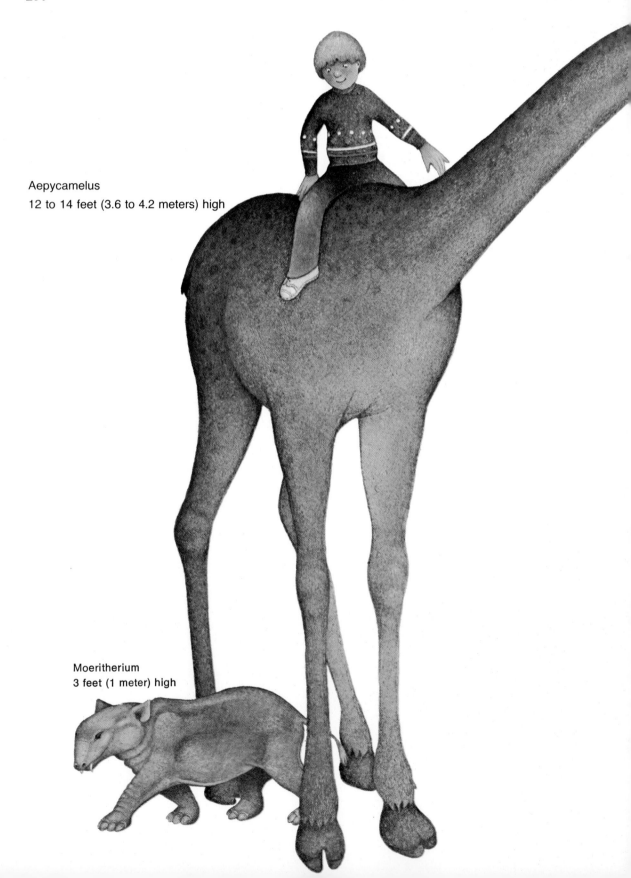

Aepycamelus
12 to 14 feet (3.6 to 4.2 meters) high

Moeritherium
3 feet (1 meter) high

How big were they?

Prehistoric mammals came in many sizes, just as mammals do now. *Moeritherium* was about the size of a hog. *Glyptodon* was about as long as a cow. *Aepycamelus* was nearly as tall as a giraffe.

Glyptodon
9 feet (2.7 meters) long

Baluchitherium
18 feet (5.4 meters) high

How big were they?

Baluchitherium, of twenty million years ago, was the biggest land mammal that has ever lived—much bigger than the biggest of all elephants. Its head was more than four feet (1.2 meters) long.

When did they live?

Most of the mammals shown on these pages lived between fifty-five million and one million years ago. But one of them, the little *Melanodon*, lived much earlier, during the time of the dinosaurs. Creatures like *Melanodon* may have been the ancestors of most of the mammals that came later.

Melanodon
135 million years ago

Oxyaena
55 million years ago

Moeritherium
35 million years ago

Ramapithecus
15 million years ago

Smilodon
1 million years ago

Uintatherium
45 million years ago

Ice Age
Animals

When the Age of Mammals began, most of the world was warm and summery all year long. But, slowly, the earth grew cooler. Huge sheets of ice, called glaciers, spread out from the North Pole and the South Pole, and from the high mountains. These great glaciers covered much of the northern and southern parts of the world about a million and a half years ago.

The lands near the glaciers were like the lands in the far north are now. There were frozen plains, and great forests of tall pine trees. Many kinds of animals lived in these lands—herds of large, shaggy mammoths, packs of wolves, rhinoceroses covered with woolly fur, and others. Human beings also lived in these cold lands and hunted many of the animals.

For many thousands of years, the earth stayed in this Ice Age. Then, the world grew warm again. The glaciers melted. But the earth's climate has changed from warm to cold and back again several times since then. The last cold time ended about ten thousand years ago.

on the next page ▶
Thirty thousand years ago, Cro-Magnon people of southern Europe hunted the giant deer and other Ice Age animals.

Helmut Diller.

The Ice Age world

A vast plain spread out beneath a dark and gloomy sky. A cold wind swirled over the plain, making the grass shiver. During the short summer, the grass had been tall and green and there had been many bright flowers. But now it was late fall. The grass was dry and yellow. The flowers were gone. Already a few small snowflakes were spinning down out of the sky, like messengers telling of terrible snowstorms that were soon to come.

There was a sound of big feet thudding rapidly on the ground. A large, shaggy animal was trotting upon the plain. This animal was as high as a tall man, and about twice as long. Two horns stuck up from its nose—a long, sharp horn in front and a shorter one behind. The creature was a huge rhinoceros, covered with thick, yellowish-brown fur.

The rhino slowed to a walk. It moved to a small, twisted birch tree, hardly bigger than a bush, and began to munch on leaves.

The sky was growing darker. Night was coming. From far in the distance, came the sound of a long, drawn-out howling. A pack of wolves was getting ready to go hunting. On another part of the plain, a great herd of reindeer was feeding. Their heads went up and their ears twitched when they heard the howling. Some members of the herd would become the wolves' prey that night.

The rhinoceros continued to munch upon its leaves. Suddenly it lifted its head, peering into the gloomy, thickening twilight. Something was coming. But the rhino's eyesight was not good, and it could not see the newcomer very clearly. Its nostrils quivered as it

giant deer

(continued from page 246)
sniffed the air to get the other animal's scent. After a
moment, the rhino went back to its meal. There was
nothing to fear.

The animal that soon came trotting past was
another plant-eater. It was a giant deer, a beautiful
creature, more than six feet (1.8 meters) high. Its
antlers were huge and heavy, like great spreading
tree branches. Its hoofs clip-clopped on the ground as
it sped quickly out of sight.

In the distance there came a loud trumpeting
sound. A dozen animals were moving slowly over the
plain. They were covered with shaggy, reddish-brown
hair and had trunks and great curled tusks. These
were the giants of the plain—mammoths.

The leader of the herd of mammoths was an old
animal, twelve feet (3.6 meters) high. It reached
down and pulled up a plant, which it stuffed

250

(continued from page 249)
into its mouth. These big creatures ate grass, herbs, and flowers. When snow was thick on the ground, the mammoths used their tusks to sweep it aside. In this way, they uncovered clumps of moss, which they ate.

The woolly rhinoceros finished its meal of leaves. It turned and trotted away. This part of the plain was its regular "territory." The rhino had made several paths as it moved about from place to place. Now it was following one of those paths to a nearby stream.

Suddenly, the earth gave way beneath the rhino's

mammoth

heavy body! It went crashing down into a shallow pit. Snorting and stamping in fear and anger, the rhino tried to climb out of the pit. But it could not. It was trapped.

The rhino had become the prey of the most dangerous creatures that hunted on the plain—humans! They had watched the rhino, and seen it use its paths. They had dug this pit in one of the paths. Soon they would come with spears. The rhinoceros meat would feed them for several days.

The hunters of the woolly rhinoceros are called Neanderthal (nee AN duhr thawl) people. They lived in Europe and in many other parts of the world from about ninety thousand to thirty-five thousand years ago. They also hunted many of the other kinds of creatures that lived in the cold, frozen lands at the edge of the glaciers—even the huge mammoths!

Many other kinds of animals also lived on the plains, in the forests, and in caves near the ice sheets. There were big cave bears, much like the great grizzly bears of today. There were also cave leopards and cave lions. Big bison roamed the forests, and herds of musk oxen plodded over the plains. There were also rabbits, foxes, and many other small animals.

Woolly rhinos, mammoths, and some of those other animals have become extinct. But many of the kinds of animals that live in the Far North today are just like those that lived in the cold lands long ago.

cave bear

Pictures from the past

Many thousands of years ago, prehistoric people
made pictures and carvings of the Ice Age animals they
saw and hunted. You can see these pictures today
on the walls of caves in France and Spain. Some are
painted in bright colors. Others are scratched into the

These paintings of prehistoric animals in Lascaux Cave in France were made more than fifteen thousand years ago. The cave was discovered in 1940 by two young boys out with their dog.

254

(continued from page 252)
stone. The carvings the people did are usually on tools made of bone.

Many of those Ice Age animals are now gone from the world, forever. But we know what they looked like because of the beautiful paintings and carvings made by those long-ago people.

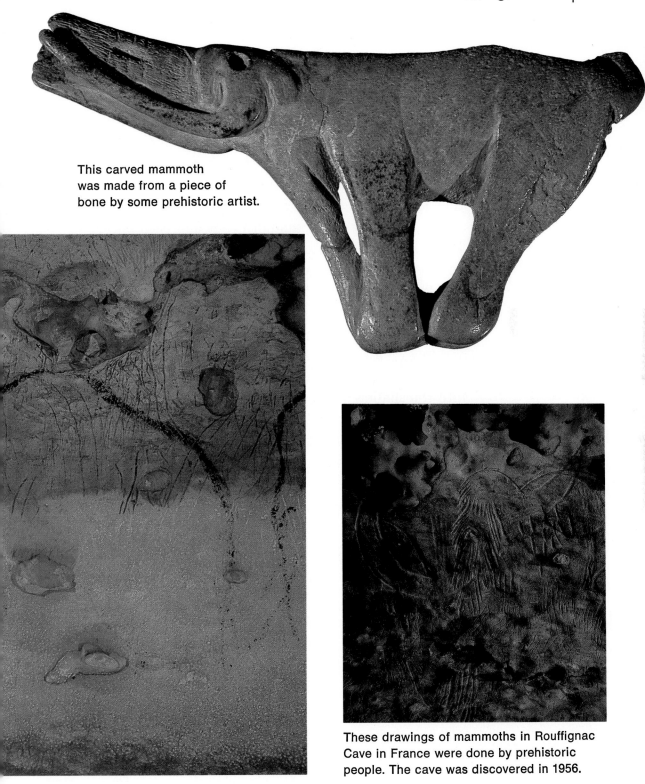

This carved mammoth was made from a piece of bone by some prehistoric artist.

These drawings of mammoths in Rouffignac Cave in France were done by prehistoric people. The cave was discovered in 1956.

A mammoth in cold storage

In the summer of 1900, a Russian hunter followed an elk along a river in Siberia. Suddenly, the hunter's dog went wild with excitement. It rushed away. The hunter followed it and came upon an amazing sight.

The dog was standing before a huge, shaggy shape that looked as if it were pushing up out of the earth. It was the body of a mammoth that had been buried in the ground for nearly forty thousand years! And it was perfectly preserved!

How had the mammoth been preserved for all those years? This is probably what happened. One autumn day, thousands of years ago, the mammoth had been walking on a riverbank. Suddenly, the bank collapsed beneath the mammoth's weight. The mammoth fell into the shallow water. Tons of dirt and stone from the bank fell on top of it.

The mammoth might have been able to push its way out, but it could not move. It had broken its hip and one of its legs when it fell. Buried under all that soil, the mammoth could not breathe. It quickly died.

Autumn in Siberia is quite cold, and winters there are terrible. The soil on top of the mammoth froze. Before long, it was covered with a thick white blanket of snow. The mammoth's body froze hard as stone.

In the spring, rain and melting snow washed more soil from the riverbank down onto the big pile of dirt that covered the mammoth. Buried under the dirt, the mammoth's body stayed frozen. And, each spring, a little more soil from the bank was washed down over the mammoth, burying it ever deeper.

After thousands of years, the whole riverbank had been washed away. Now, each spring, rain and melting snow carried away some of the soil that covered the mammoth. Finally, after thousands of more years,

(continued from page 257)
great rains washed away the last of the soil and the mammoth's body was uncovered. That was when the hunter's dog smelled it and found it.

Nearly a year went by before Russian scientists heard of the discovery. They then quickly sent an expedition to Siberia, which is in the part of Russia that is in Asia. But it took the men four months to reach the mammoth's body. By this time the body had begun to rot. And it had been partly eaten by wolves and other animals. Even so, there was still enough of it left for the scientists to learn a great deal from it.

They found out what kinds of food the big mammoth ate from the remains in its stomach. And they found that beneath its long, reddish-brown hair its body was covered with woolly, yellowish fur. This fur must have helped to keep the animal warm during the fierce Siberian winters.

The scientists took the mammoth's skin and all of the bones back home with them. Later, the mammoth was put on display. It can be seen today in the Zoological Museum at the University of Leningrad.

The frozen remains of about fifty other mammoths have been found in Siberia and Alaska. And the remains of woolly rhinos, still covered with fur, have also been found in Siberia. These wonderful finds have helped us to learn much more about these creatures of the Ice Age.

Two Russian children view the mammoth found
frozen in Siberia. Now in a museum in Leningrad,
it is shown just as it looked when it was found.

How big were they?

The woolly rhinoceros of the Ice Age was about the same size as a rhino of today. The mammoth was a little bigger than a modern elephant.

woolly rhinoceros
6 feet (1.8 meters) high

mammoth
12 feet (3.6 meters) high

Neanderthal man
90,000 years ago

Mammoth
60,000 years ago

Woolly rhinoceros, 60,000 years ago

When did they live?

These animals and men of the Ice Age lived between ninety thousand and twenty-five thousand years ago. The Neanderthal people, who were probably the ancestors of the Cro-Magnon people, hunted animals such as mammoths, woolly rhinos, and cave bears for food and clothing. The Cro-Magnons, who were people just like us, hunted mostly reindeer and elk.

Cave bear
60,000
years ago

Cro-Magnon man
35,000 years ago

Giant deer
25,000 years ago

The Past
in the Present

Dinosaurs, mammoths, and all the other prehistoric animals have long been gone from the earth. And yet, these creatures of the past are part of our lives today.

You can go into any big museum in the world and see fossils and models of these animals of long ago. Sometimes you can find life-sized statues of these creatures in parks and playgrounds.

You can go into any library and you will find dozens of books about prehistoric life. There have been movies and television programs in which prehistoric animals were the "stars." And, of course, there are a great many prehistoric animal toys, games, and puzzles.

People have a tremendous interest in prehistoric animals. That's why we bring them out of the past and into the present in as many ways as we can.

on the next page ▶
Children watch as a sculptor makes a life-sized model of the meat-eating dinosaur *Tyrannosaurus* for a museum.

The bone hunters

For several days, a small group of people has been traveling through rough, rocky desert. They are searching for the bones of prehistoric animals. These people are all scientists who work for a museum. They know the kinds of places where there may be fossil bones. But even so, the bones are often hard to find.

(continued on page 270)

These scientists have discovered a dinosaur bone in a rocky desert. They know there are probably more bones buried beneath this one.

A bulldozer is used to remove the upper
layer of soil and rock so that scientists
can get the buried bones out more easily.

As soon as a fossil bone is dug up, it must be coated with shellac. The shellac hardens the bone and helps to protect it.

(continued from page 268)

Suddenly, one of the scientists notices something. To most people, what he sees might look like any ordinary chunk of rock. But his trained eyes can recognize part of a fossil bone sticking up out of a rocky ridge. And he knows that where there is one bone, there are probably others.

Now begins the hard work beneath the hot, desert sun. The scientists carefully remove the fossil bones from the rock they are buried in. Each bone is then carefully wrapped and protected against damage.

Weeks later, the bones are back in the museum, ready for study. Perhaps they will reveal something new about the animals of long ago.

Strips of cloth soaked in wet plaster are wrapped around the bone. The plaster dries rock hard, protecting the bone.

The plaster-coated bone is carefully loaded onto a truck for the journey to a museum.

The skeleton builders

Fossil bones that scientists find are sent back to a museum. There, the bones are carefully cleaned. If the bones are damaged, they are repaired. As often as not, scientists find only a few bones on their field trips. But sometimes enough bones are found to make up a whole skeleton.

The work of putting together skeletons of prehistoric animals is done by people called preparators. These people are often animal experts, sculptors, artists, and mechanics all rolled into one!

Preparators have to know a lot about the bodies of animals—how the bones fit together and how the muscles work. The preparator must put a skeleton

Scientists cover the fossil bones they find with plaster, for protection. At a museum, the plaster is removed and the bones are carefully cleaned.

The bones are joined with metal rods that form a frame for the skeleton. Slowly, bone by bone, the skeleton is put together.

The finished skeleton is put on display in the museum for visitors and scientists to see.

together so that it looks just as it did when it was inside a live animal's body.

Many times some of the bones are missing. Then the preparator becomes a sculptor, making new bones out of plaster or plastic. The false bones are usually colored to look like real ones.

The bones of prehistoric animals are as heavy as rock. So they have to be held together by a very sturdy metal frame. The preparators have to plan and build the frame. Then they fit the skeleton on it, a little at a time.

Putting the skeleton of a prehistoric animal together is hard work. But it sounds like fun!

Skeletons on display

After the skeleton of a prehistoric animal is finally put together, it usually goes on display in the museum. There, you and others can come to look at it. If you have ever seen such a skeleton, you know what a sight it is. Just think, you are looking at the last remains of a creature that lived millions of years ago.

This skeleton of a tyrannosaur was found in Alberta, Canada. It is now on display at the National Museum of Natural Sciences, Ottawa.

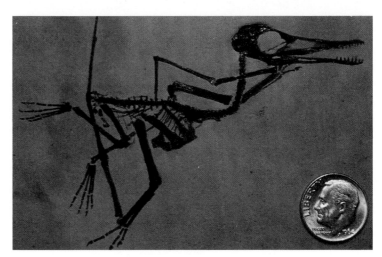

Pterodactylus, the smallest
flying reptile known, was
about the size of a canary.
This skeleton, compared
to a dime, can be seen at
Harvard University, Boston.

Part of the fossil skeleton of a prehistoric armored
amphibian in a museum at Harvard University.

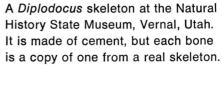

A *Diplodocus* skeleton at the Natural History State Museum, Vernal, Utah. It is made of cement, but each bone is a copy of one from a real skeleton.

The skeleton of a *Stegosaurus* at the Smithsonian Institution, Washington, D.C. The large, pointed plates on its back may have helped to protect it.

The skull of a meat-eating tyrannosaur at the National Museum of Natural Sciences, Ottawa, Canada. The skull is four feet (1.2 meters) long and the teeth are six inches (15 cm) long.

This skeleton of a prehistoric elephant called *Archidiskodon* (ahr kee DIHS kuh dahn) is at the University of Nebraska at Lincoln. It stands about fourteen feet (4.2 meters) high at the shoulder.

Making a dinosaur model

Many museums display fine models of prehistoric animals. The models are made by artists and sculptors, working closely with scientists. The pictures on these pages show how a life-sized model of *Allosaurus*, a meat-eating dinosaur, was made for the Museum of the University of Nebraska.

1 First, artists make drawings of all the parts of the *Allosaurus*'s skeleton.

2 A small model is made. The model and drawings are used as guides when making the life-sized "skeleton" out of metal beams and wire.

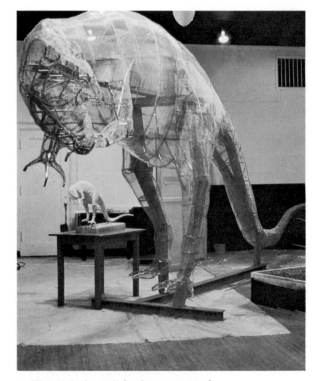

3 The "skeleton" is then covered with a "skin" of fine wire screen.

4 The completed "skeleton," now looking very much like the small model, is ready for a coat of plaster.

5 The wire mesh is covered with plaster. Scales and skin folds are then worked into the plaster.

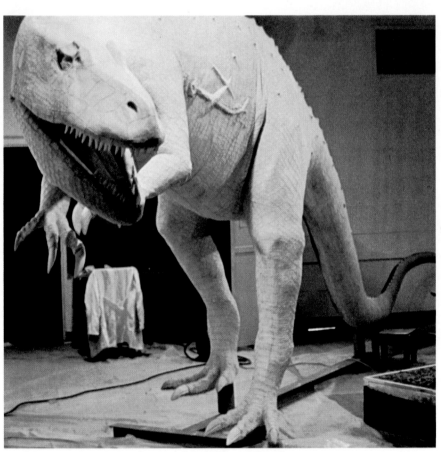

6 Now the finished model is ready to be painted. Turn the page and you will see how it looks on display in the museum.

This is the life-sized model of *Allosaurus* that you saw being made on pages 278–279. Now finished, it is on display at the University of Nebraska at Lincoln.

A life-sized model of a prehistoric elephant trapped in the
La Brea tar pits, Hancock Park, Los Angeles. About a million
fossils of Ice Age animals have been found here.

Monster models

It's fun to look at the skeletons of huge
dinosaurs. But it's even more fun to look
at a model of a dinosaur, especially when
the model is as big as the animal really
was. Such models show, better than any
other way, what those big, awesome
animals of long ago probably looked like
when they were alive.

This diorama at the American Museum
of Natural History in New York shows
Protoceratops hatching from eggs.

Everybody loves a dinosaur!

All the dinosaurs have been dead for millions of years. But these creatures are almost as much a part of the world now as they were when they were alive!

Reminders of dinosaurs are all around us. You often see them in movies and on television. There are also hundreds of books about them. And you'll sometimes find models or statues of them in parks, playgrounds, and public places.

People have been interested in these big, strange creatures ever since they were first discovered. It's not surprising that pictures, models, and statues of them turn up in all sorts of places. So wherever you go, look around—there may be a dinosaur nearby!

Dinosaurs were the "stars" in the Walt Disney movie *Fantasia.*

These children are having fun playing on a model *Triceratops.*

The sculptor who made this fun statue of a *Stegosaurus* used an automobile for the body!

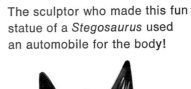

Let's make a dinosaur

What could be more fun than to make your very own dinosaur?

Here are some prehistoric animals that were built by children—from miniature dinosaurs made of clay to a life-sized dinosaur skeleton made of cardboard. Perhaps they will give you some ideas for making your own prehistoric animals.

To make this parade of prehistoric creatures, children used such things as clay, toothpicks, beads, yarn, cloves, pistachio nut shells, and cupcake molds.

This life-sized cardboard skeleton of the dinosaur *Stegosaurus* was made by children in Australia.

A dinosaur diorama

A diorama is a small, real-looking scene made with model plants, animals, and scenery. You can build a diorama in a small box, such as a shoe box. For the background, use a magazine picture of distant trees or mountains. Paste the picture on the inside back and sides of the box. Then put in your model plants, rocks, and animals.

You can use all kinds of things to make a diorama. You can make plants out of paper, cloth, clay—or use real weeds. A pencil wrapped in crepe paper makes a good trunk for a palm tree. For rocks, use real rocks, big seeds, or sea shells. For ideas on making animals, see pages 284–285.

Six Hundred Million Years of Life

Scientists have divided the history of the earth into vast periods of time called eras (ihr uhs). Each era is divided into shorter times called periods or epochs (ehp uhks).

Each period or epoch is represented by a layer of rock formed during that time. Scientists can tell how old rock is and how long it took to form. So each layer is a record of time. And fossils in the rock are a record of the animal and plant life that lived when the rock was forming.

The chart below lists the time periods and shows about when each began and ended. It also shows some animals and plants that lived in each period. The chart is arranged like the layers of rock in the earth, with the oldest period at the bottom. So the chart should be read from the bottom up.

The time periods are explained on the next five pages. Under each period is a list of most animals in this book whose fossils date from that time. You are given some facts about each animal and shown how to say its name. If there is a page number, you will find a picture of the animal on that page. To find out more about an animal, use the Index.

	Time Period	Began	Ended	Lasted	Animal and Plant Life
Cenozoic Era	Holocene Epoch	10,000 years ago	Not yet ended	Not yet ended	Humans; farm animals; farm plants
	Pleistocene Epoch	1,750,000 years ago	10,000 years ago	1,740,000 years	Early humans; mammoths; modern plants
	Pliocene Epoch	14 million years ago	1,750,000 years ago	12,250,000 years	First humans; modern birds and fish
	Miocene Epoch	26 million years ago	14 million years ago	12 million years	Many mammals; flowering plants and trees
	Oligocene Epoch	40 million years ago	26 million years ago	14 million years	First apes; early elephants; huge rhinoceroslike animals
	Eocene Epoch	55 million years ago	40 million years ago	15 million years	First horses, camels, whales, and rhinoceroses
	Paleocene Epoch	65 million years ago	55 million years ago	10 million years	Many small mammals; flowering plants common
Mesozoic Era	Cretaceous Period	130 million years ago	65 million years ago	65 million years	Horned and armored dinosaurs; flowering plants
	Jurassic Period	180 million years ago	130 million years ago	50 million years	Huge dinosaurs; first birds; many cone-bearing trees
	Triassic Period	225 million years ago	180 million years ago	45 million years	First dinosaurs, turtles, crocodiles, and mammals
Paleozoic Era	Permian Period	275 million years ago	225 million years ago	50 million years	Many reptiles; first seed plants—cone-bearing trees
	Carboniferous Period	345 million years ago	275 million years ago	70 million years	First reptiles; many huge swampy forests
	Devonian Period	405 million years ago	345 million years ago	60 million years	Many fish; first amphibians and insects; first forests
	Silurian Period	435 million years ago	405 million years ago	30 million years	First air-breathing animals; first land plants
	Ordovician Period	480 million years ago	435 million years ago	45 million years	Many trilobites and shelled animals; first jawless fish
	Cambrian Period	600 million years ago	480 million years ago	120 million years	Trilobites common; first large number of fossils
Precambrian Time		4,600,000,000 years ago	600 million years ago	4 billion years	Very few fossils

Precambrian Time

Precambrian (pree KAM bree uhn) Time, the first four billion years in the history of the earth, ended about 600 million years ago.

Precambrian means "before the Cambrian Period." It was during Precambrian Time that life began in the sea. However, the rocks from that time contain few fossils.

Paleozoic Era

The Paleozoic (pay lee uh ZOH ihk) Era lasted for 375 million years—from 600 million to 225 million years ago. The name *Paleozoic* means "ancient life." This era is divided into six periods.

Cambrian Period The Cambrian (KAM bree uhn) Period lasted for 120 million years —from 600 million to 480 million years ago. *Cambria* was the Roman name for Wales, where rock formed during this period was first found. In the Cambrian, there was no life on the land. But the water was full of life.

brachiopod (BRAK ee uh pahd), 52
   A brachiopod is a small, soft, clamlike water animal with a hinged shell.

jellyfish (JEHL ee fihsh), 42
   This water animal has a jellylike body.
onychophoran (ahn uh KAHF uh ruhn), 43
   These animals look rather like caterpillars.
sponge (spuhnj), 43
   This water animal looks like a plant.
trilobite (TRY luh byt), 48
   A trilobite was a water animal.
trilobitomorph (try luh BYT uh mawrf), 42
   Trilobitomorphs were like trilobites.

Ordovician Period The Ordovician (awr duh VIHSH uhn) Period lasted for 45 million years —from 480 million to 435 million years ago. This rock layer is named for an ancient tribe that lived in Wales. During the Ordovician, small, fishlike creatures with backbones appeared. And, very slowly, plants started to move from the water to the land.

cephalopod (SEHF uh luh pahd), 50
   A cephalopod is a water animal with long tentacles and large eyes.

coral polyp (KAWR uhl PAHL ihp), 52
   A coral polyp is a tiny water animal with a sacklike body and tentacles. These small animals live in cuplike shells that are joined together to make pieces of coral.
crinoid (KRY noyd), 53
   A crinoid is a water animal that looks like a lily.
graptolite (GRAP tuh lyt), 53
   A graptolite was a tiny water animal with a cuplike shell.

Silurian Period The Silurian (suh LUR ee uhn) Period lasted for 30 million years —from 435 million to 405 million years ago. The Period was named for the Silures, an ancient tribe that lived in Wales where this layer of rock was first found. During this period, true land plants appeared and some water animals moved to the land.

eurypterid (yu RIHP tuhr ihd), 66
   A eurypterid was a water animal that looked like a scorpion. The name means "broad-winged."

ostracoderm (AHS truh koh durm), 66
   An ostracoderm was a jawless, fishlike animal with a bony shell on its head and back. The name means "shell skin."
Palaeophonus (pay lee uh FOHN uhs), 72
   Palaeophonus was a kind of scorpion. It is believed to have been the first animal to leave the water and live on land.

Devonian Period The Devonian (duh VOH nee uhn) Period lasted for 60 million years —from 405 million to 345 million years ago. It is named for Devonshire, England. The Devonian is often called the "Age of Fishes" because there were so many kinds of fish. The first amphibians and the first forests appeared during this period.

acanthodian (ack uhn THOH dee uhn), 57
   An acanthodian was a small fish.

ammonite (AM uh nyt), 176
   An ammonite was an octopuslike creature with a coiled shell, like that of a snail.
coelacanth (SEE luh kanth), 63
   This fish is often called a "living fossil."
Eusthenopteron (yoos thehn AHP tuhr ahn), 70
   This fish may have been able to live and walk on land for short periods of time.
fringe-fin (frihnj fihn), 59
   This kind of fish had stubby fins. The

Devonian Period (continued)
coelacanth and *Eusthenopteron* were fringe-fins.
giant armored fish, 61
This huge, prehistoric fish had bony armor.
Ichthyostega (ikh thee uh STAY guh), 74
Ichthyostega was the first amphibian.

ray-fin (ray fihn), 58
These fish have strips of bone in their fins.
shark (shahrk), 61
The ancient sharks that lived in Devonian seas were much like modern sharks.
Terataspis (tehr uh TAS pihs), 67
This water animal was a giant trilobite.

Carboniferous Period The Carboniferous (kahr buh NIHF uhr uhs) Period lasted for 70 million years—from 345 million to 275 million years ago. The name means "carbon (coal) forming." In this period, many of today's coal beds began to form where there were huge, swampy forests. Amphibians and insects were the main land animals, but the first reptiles appeared near the end of the Carboniferous Period.
Diplovertebron (dihp luh VUHR tuh brahn), 80
Diplovertebron was a small amphibian.

Eogyrinus (ee oh jy RIHN uhs), 78
This animal was a large amphibian, somewhat like a giant salamander.
Hylonomus (hy LAHN uh muhs), 88
Hylonomus was an early reptile.
Meganeura (mehg uh NUR uh), 83
Meganeura was a giant dragonfly.
Ophiderpeton (oh fih DUHR peh tahn), 85
This animal was a legless amphibian.
Romeriscus (roh muhr IS kuhs), 90
Romeriscus is the earliest reptile known from a fossil.

Permian Period The Permian (PUR mee uhn) Period lasted for 50 million years—from 275 million to 225 million years ago. It is named for the province of Perm in Russia. The first seed plants—cone-bearing trees—appeared and there were many reptiles. Trilobites and eurypterids died out near the end of the period.
Bradysaurus (bra dee SAWR uhs), 109
Bradysaurus was a big, plant-eating reptile.

Dimetrodon (dy MEH truh dahn), 97
This reptile was a four-footed meat-eater.
Edaphosaurus (ee daf uh SAWR uhs), 108
This reptile was a four-footed plant-eater.
Lycaenops (LY kayn ahps), 106
Lycaenops was a meat-eating reptile.
Mesosaurus (mehs uh SAWR uhs), 95
Mesosaurus was a small, slim water reptile.
Moschops (MAH skahps), 108
This reptile was a four-footed plant-eater.

Mesozoic Era
The Mesozoic (mehs uh ZOH ihk) Era lasted for 160 million years—from 225 million to 65 million years ago. *Mesozoic* means "middle

life." This era (together with the earlier Permian Period) is often called the "Age of Reptiles." The Mesozoic Era is divided into three periods.

Triassic Period The Triassic (try AS ihk) Period lasted for 45 million years—from 225 million to 180 million years ago. The name *Triassic* refers to the three different kinds of rocks found in the layer that formed at that time. It was during the Triassic Period that turtles, crocodiles, dinosaurs, and mammals first appeared.
Coelophysis (see LOH fuh sihs), 120
Coelophysis was one of the first dinosaurs.
Cynognathus (sihn uh NATH uhs), 102
This reptile may have been covered with fur instead of scales.
Henodus (HEHN oh duhs), 167
This large water reptile had a shell much like that of a turtle.

Ornithosuchus (awr nuh thuh SOOK uhs), 113
This large reptile was an early dinosaur.
phytosaur (FY tuh sawr), 170
These water reptiles were like crocodiles.
Plateosaurus (plat ee uh SAWR uhs), 121
This animal was a large dinosaur that walked on its hind legs.
rhynchosaur (RIHNG koh sawr), 175
These reptiles looked like lizards. They were four-footed reptiles with snouts like beaks.
Teratosaurus (tehr uh tuh SAWR uhs) This large dinosaur was a meat-eater.
thecodont (THEE kuh dahnt), 105
These small reptiles were the ancestors of the dinosaurs.

Jurassic Period The Jurassic (ju RAS ihk) Period lasted for 50 million years—from 180 million to 130 million years ago. The period is named for the Jura Mountains between France and Switzerland. The first birds appeared during the Jurassic Period.

Allosaurus (al uh SAWR uhs), 280
Allosaurus was a very large, two-footed, meat-eating dinosaur.

Apatosaurus (ap uh tuh SAWR uhs), 184
This dinosaur is also called *Brontosaurus*.

Archaeopteryx (ahr kee AHP tuhr ihks), 172
This animal is the first known bird.

Brachiosaurus (brak ee uh SAWR uhs)
Brachiosaurus was one of the biggest of the four-footed, plant-eating dinosaurs.

Brontosaurus (brahn tuh SAWR uhs)
This is another name for *Apatosaurus*.

Camarasaurus (kam uh ruh SAWR uhs)
This enormous dinosaur was a plant-eater.

Camptosaurus (kamp tuh SAWR uhs), 146
This dinosaur was a plant-eater.

Ceratosaurus (sehr uh tuh SAWR uhs)
This large dinosaur had a horn on its nose.

Compsognathus (kahmp SAHG nuh thuhs), 133
This dinosaur was the smallest one known.

Dimorphodon (dy MAWR fuh dahn), 163
Dimorphodon was a flying reptile.

Diplodocus (duh PLAHD uh kuhs)
Diplodocus was a plant-eating dinosaur.

ichthyosaur (IHK thee uh sawr), 160
These water reptiles looked like dolphins.

Kentrosaurus (kehn truh SAWR uhs)
This large dinosaur was a plant-eater.

Megalosaurus (mehg uh luh SAWR uhs)
This large dinosaur was a meat-eater.

Melanodon (mehl AN uh dahn), 240
Melanodon was an early mammal that was much like the modern shrew.

Ornitholestes (awr nuh thuh LEHS teez), 123
This small dinosaur was a meat-eater.

plesiosaur (PLEE see uh sawr), 159
Plesiosaurs were water reptiles. Some had long necks and others had short necks.

Pterodactylus (tehr uh DAK tuh luhs), 162
Pterodactylus was a small, flying reptile.

Rhamphorhynchus (ram fuh RIHNG kuhs), 162
This animal was a small, flying reptile.

Scelidosaurus (sehl uh duh SAWR uhs)
This animal was an early, plated dinosaur

Stegosaurus (stehg uh SAWR uhs), 140
Stegosaurus was a large, plated dinosaur.

Cretaceous Period The Cretaceous (krih TAY shuhs) Period lasted for 65 million years—from 130 million to 65 million years ago. *Cretaceous* means "chalky," and refers to the chalk formed during this period. The dinosaurs died out by the end of the Cretaceous Period.

Acanthopholis (uh kan thuh FOH lihs)
Acanthopholis was an armored dinosaur.

Albertosaurus (al bur tuh SAWR uhs)
Albertosaurus was a very large meat-eating dinosaur that had tiny front legs.

Anatosaurus (uh nat uh SAWR uhs), 151
This creature was a duckbilled dinosaur.

Ankylosaurus (ang kuh luh SAWR uhs)
Ankylosaurus was an armored dinosaur.

Archelon (AHR kuh lahn), 168
Archelon was a giant sea turtle.

Cheneosaurus (kee nee uh SAWR uhs)
Cheneosaurus was a duckbilled dinosaur.

Corythosaurus (kuh rihth uh SAWR uhs), 152
This duckbilled dinosaur had a bony head crest shaped like a half circle.

Deinonychus (dy NAHN ee kuhs), 135
This dinosaur was a small meat-eater.

Elasmosaurus (ih laz muh SAWR uhs), 181
This reptile was a plesiosaur (PLEE see uh sawr) with a very long neck.

Gryposaurus (grihp uh SAWR uhs)
This large, duckbilled dinosaur had a bony bump on its nose.

Hesperornis (hehs puh RAWR nihs), 174
Hesperornis was a large swimming bird.

Hylaeosaurus (hy lee uh SAWR uhs), 144
This dinosaur had spikes on its back and tail.

Iguanodon (ih GWAHN uh dahn), 149
Iguanodon was a large, two-legged, plant-eating reptile.

Kronosaurus (krohn uh SAWR uhs)
This animal was a very large sea reptile.

Lambeosaurus (lam bee uh SAWR uhs), 153
This large, duckbilled dinosaur had a bony head crest that resembled an ax.

Monoclonius (mehn uh KLOH nee uhs), 181
This dinosaur had a horn on its nose.

mosasaur (MOH suh sawr)
These animals were large sea lizards that had flippers instead of legs.

Pachycephalosaurus
    (pak uh sehf uh luh SAWR uhs)
This large dinosaur was a plant-eater.

Pachyrhinosaurus (pak uh ryn uh SAWR uhs)
This dinosaur had a bony knob on its nose.

(continued on page 292)

Cretaceous Period (continued)
Palaeoscincus (pay lee uh SKINK uhs), 145
  Palaeoscincus was an armored dinosaur.
Parasaurolophus
  (par uh sawr AWL uh fuhs), 153
  Parasaurolophus was a duckbilled
  dinosaur.
Pentaceratops (pehn tuh SEHR uh tahps)
  Pentaceratops was a five-horned
  dinosaur.
Pinacosaurus (pin acko SAWR uhs)
  Pinacosaurus was an armored dinosaur.
Protoceratops (proh toh SEHR uh tahps)
  This small dinosaur had no horns, but is
  part of the horned dinosaur group.

Pteranodon (tehr AN uh dahn), 163
  Pteranodon was a large, flying reptile.
Quetzalcoatlus (keht sahl koh AN tuhl uhs)
  Quetzalcoatlus, a flying reptile, was the
  largest winged creature we know of.
Spinosaurus (spyn uh SAWR uhs)
  This dinosaur had a big fin on its back.
Struthiomimus (stroo thee oh MY muhs), 134
  This dinosaur looked rather like an ostrich.
Styracosaurus (sty rak uh SAWR uhs), 156
  Styracosaurus was a horned dinosaur.
Triceratops (try SEHR uh tahps), 185
  This dinosaur had three horns on its head.
Tyrannosaurus (tih ran uh SAWR uhs), 137
  This dinosaur was large and savage-looking.

Cenozoic Era
The Cenozoic (see nuh ZOH ihk) Era is the era
we are living in now. This era began 65 million
years ago and has not yet ended. *Cenozoic*
means "new life," a name that refers to the
many new kinds of life that developed during
this time. The Cenozoic Era is divided into
seven epochs (EHP uhks).

Paleocene Epoch The Paleocene (PAY lee uh
seen) Epoch lasted for 10 million years—from
65 million to 55 million years ago. *Paleocene*
means "ancient new." During this epoch,
mammals spread out and took the place
of reptiles as rulers of the earth.
Barylambda (bar uh LAM duh), 188
  This big, powerful animal was an early
  mammal. Its name refers to the shape of
  some of its teeth.

Eocene Epoch The Eocene (EE uh seen)
Epoch lasted for 15 million years—from 55
million to 40 million years ago. *Eocene* means
"dawn of the new." It was during the Eocene
that the ancestors of many modern mammals
appeared.
Basilosaurus (bas uh luh SAWR uhs), 193
  This animal was an early whale.
Coryphodon (kuh RIHF uh dahn), 197
  Coryphodon looked like a hippopotamus.
creodont (KREE uh dahnt), 195
  Creodonts were the first hunting mammals.
Diatryma (dy uh TRY muh), 28
  Diatryma was a large bird that could not fly.

Eohippus (ee oh HIHP uhs), 204
  Eohippus was the first kind of horse.
  It is also known as *Hyracotherium*.
Hyracotherium (hy ruh koh THIHR ee uhm), 204
  This is another name for *Eohippus*.
miacid (MY uh sihd)
  Miacids were the ancestors of dogs and cats.
Notharctus (nuh THAHRK tuhs), 198
  This small, furry animal was an ancestor of
  the monkey.
Oxyaena (ahk see EE nuh), 197
  This mammal was one kind of creodont.
Uintatherium (yoo ihn tuh THIHR ee uhm), 192
  Uintatherium had six horns on its head.

Oligocene Epoch The Oligocene (AHL uh goh
seen) Epoch lasted for 14 million years—from
40 million to 26 million years ago. *Oligocene*
means "few of the new." Many modern
mammals appeared during that time.
Aegyptopithecus
  (ee jihp tuh PIHTH uh kus), 210
  This animal may be the ancestor of apes.
Arsinoitherium
  (ahr sih noy THIHR ee uhm), 200
  This large mammal had two huge horns.

Brontotherium (brahn tuh THIHR ee uhm), 208
  This mammal had a Y-shaped nose horn.
  Its name means "thunder beast."
Mesohippus (mehs oh HIHP uhs), 205
  Mesohippus, or "middle horse," was about
  the size of a large dog.
moerithere (MIHR uh thihr), 213
  These small, long-nosed mammals were the
  ancestors of the elephants.
Phiomia (fy OH mee uh), 214
  Phiomia was a kind of elephant.

Miocene Epoch The Miocene (MY uh seen) Epoch lasted for 12 million years—from 26 million to 14 million years ago. The name *Miocene* means "less new." During the Miocene, grasses became widespread and grass-eating animals became numerous.

Aepycamelus (eh pi kuh MEE luhs), 236
This tall camel looked like a giraffe.

Baluchitherium
(buh loo chuh THIHR ee uhm), 220
This enormous, hornless rhinoceros was the biggest of all land mammals.

deinotherium (dy nuh THIHR ee uhm), 215
A deinotherium was a kind of elephant with down-curving tusks in its lower jaw.

Dryopithecus (dry uh PIHTH uh kuhs)
Dryopithecus was an ape.

Merychippus (mehr ih KIHP uhs)
Merychippus, or "grass-eating" horse, was about the size of a sheep.

Moropus (MAWR uh puhs), 201
Moropus looked somewhat like a large horse, but had claws instead of hoofs.

Phororhacos (foh RAWR uh kuhs), 202
This large, meat-eating bird could not fly.

Platybelodon (plat ee BEHL uh dahn), 216
This animal was a kind of elephant.

Ramapithecus (ram uh PIHTH uh kuhs), 212
This apelike creature may have been the ancestor of modern apes and humans.

Stenomylus (stehn uh MY luhs), 223
Stenomylus was a fast-running camel.

Procamelus (proh kuh MEE luhs), 224
Procamelus was the first modern camel.

Pliocene Epoch The Pliocene (PLY uh seen) Epoch lasted for more than 12 million years—from 14 million to 1,750,000 years ago. *Pliocene* means "more recent." In this epoch, the first humans appeared and many mammals moved from one continent to another.

Teleoceras (tehl ee AHS uhr uhs), 219
Teleoceras, or "end horn," was a short-legged rhinoceros that had a very short horn on its nose.

Pleistocene Epoch The Pleistocene (PLYS tuh seen) Epoch lasted for almost two million years—from 1,750,000 to 10,000 years ago. *Pleistocene* means "most recent." This epoch is often called the "Ice Age," because several times during those years parts of the earth were covered with glaciers. Modern humans appeared near the end of this epoch.

cave bear, 251
A cave bear looked like a grizzly bear.

Cro-Magnon (kroh MAG nahn), 263
The Cro-Magnon people appeared about thirty-five thousand years ago. They are named for the cave in France where their skeletons were first found.

Diprotodon (dy PROH tuh dahn), 229
Diprotodon was a four-footed marsupial.

giant deer, 248
This animal had enormous antlers. Many fossils of this animal have been found in Ireland.

Glyptodon (GLIHP tuh dahn), 232
This mammal had a bony, armorlike shell. Its name means "carved tooth."

mammoth (MAM uhth), 250
Mammoths were large, furry elephants. They appeared about four million years ago.

mastodon (MAS tuh dahn), 217
Mastodons were ancient relatives of the elephant. They appeared about forty million years ago and became extinct some eight thousand years ago.

Megatherium (mehg uh THIHR ee uhm), 234
This animal was a giant ground sloth.

Neanderthal (nee AN duhr thawl), 262
The Neanderthal people lived between one hundred thousand and thirty-five thousand years ago. They are named for the Neander Valley in Germany, where their fossils were first found.

short-faced kangaroo, 227
This animal was a very large kangaroo.

Smilodon (SMY luh dahn), 230
Smilodon, also called a *saber-toothed tiger*, had two very long, sharp teeth.

woolly rhinoceros
(WUL ee ry NAHS uhr uhs), 247
This animal had thick, woolly fur.

Holocene Epoch The Holocene (HAHL uh seen) Epoch is the epoch we are living in today. It began about 10,000 years ago. No one knows how long this epoch will last.

Holocene means "completely new." During the Holocene Epoch, people have learned how to raise animals and crops, invented writing, and even traveled to the moon.

Books to Read

There are many good books about prehistoric animals and the prehistoric world for readers of all ages. A few are listed here. Your school or public library will have some of these, as well as many others.

Ages 5 to 8

Digging Up Dinosaurs by Aliki (Crowell, 1988)
Cartoon-style pictures show how scientists find fossils, dig them up, and prepare them for display in museums.

Dinosaurs and Their World by Laurence Pringle (Harcourt, 1976)
Carefully written and well illustrated, this dinosaur book is one of the best. The text describes the world of the dinosaurs, as well as field work and the preparation of fossils for exhibits. Included is a list of museums in North America that have dinosaur exhibits. Although an upper-level book for this age group, it is one that good readers with an interest in the subject will enjoy.

Dinosaur Time by Peggy Parish (Scholastic, 1989)
This is a good book for the young reader. It features large print and short, simple sentences. A number of dinosaurs are pictured.

Fossils Tell of Long Ago by Aliki (Harcourt, 1983)
Colorful illustrations and easy-to-read text explain what fossils are and how they were formed. The reader is shown how to make a one-minute-old "fossil" to further help in understanding how fossilization takes place.

Strange Creatures That Really Lived by Millicent Ellis Selsam (Scholastic, 1987)
An excellent introduction to some of the creatures that lived long ago. Easy-to-read text and pleasing illustrations add to this book's charm.

Whatever Happened to the Dinosaurs? by Bernard Most (Harcourt, 1988)
An attempt to answer this question uncovers some possible and some impossible explanations. Colorful, funny illustrations complement the text. Also by the same author: *If the Dinosaurs Came Back* and *Dinosaur Cousins?*

Ages 9-12

Album of Dinosaurs by Tom McGowen (Macmillan, 1987)
A number of dinosaurs are illustrated and discussed in full,
while others are covered to a lesser extent, in text that
combines exciting narrative with interesting facts. Also by the
same author: *Album of Prehistoric Man.*

Dinosaurs Walked Here by Patricia Lauber (Bradbury, 1987)
A fascinating look at what fossils are, how they are formed, how
they are found and studied, and what they tell about ancient
forms of life. Dramatic photographs make the information
contained in this book complete.

The Enormous Egg by Oliver Butterworth (Dell, 1987)
Nate thinks the big egg in the barn was laid by one of the hens.
Imagine his surprise when the egg hatches and it's a Triceratops!

Giants from the Past edited by Donald J. Crump (National
  Geographic Society, 1983)
An interesting book full of information about prehistoric horses,
cats, elephants, and other creatures. Photographs show how
fossils are found and put together to make skeletons.

**The Macmillan Book of Dinosaurs and Other Prehistoric
  Animals** by Mary Elting (Macmillan, 1987)
Arranged by historical time periods, this highly informative
book will be a useful addition to any collection of books on
prehistoric animals.

The New Dinosaur Dictionary by Donald F. Glut (Citadel,
  1984)
Although this book is aimed primarily at high-school-age
readers, a younger child with good reading ability and an
overwhelming interest in dinosaurs will find it a treasure-trove.
It lists virtually every known dinosaur and briefly tells
everything that is known about each. And it is chock-full of
pictures.

Trapped in Tar by Caroline Arnold (Clarion, 1987)
An exciting look at the kinds of fossils found in southern
California tar pits. Black and white photographs show how
bones are put together to reconstruct the animals.

New Words

Here are some of the words you have met in this book. Some of these words you'll know, but others may be new to you. You will see these words again, so they're good words to know. Next to each word, you'll see how to say it: algae (AL jee). The part shown in capital letters is said a little more loudly than the rest of the word. One or two sentences under each word tell you what the word means. (For the names of prehistoric animals and how to say them, turn to pages 288–293.)

algae (AL jee)
Algae are plants that do not have stems, roots, or leaves. They live in water or moist soil and make their own food.

amphibian (am FIHB ee uhn)
An amphibian is an animal that lives in water and breathes with gills when it is young. Later, it usually develops lungs and moves onto land. Frogs and toads are amphibians.

ancestor (AN sehs tuhr)
An ancestor is one from whom a living thing is descended. Your parents and grandparents are your ancestors.

billion (BIHL yuhn)
In the United States and Canada (and in this book), a billion is a thousand millions and is written 1,000,000,000. In Great Britain and Australia, a billion is a million millions and is written 1,000,000,000,000.

biped (BY pehd)
A biped is an animal that moves on two legs. People and birds are bipeds.

climate (KLY miht)
Climate is the kind of weather that a place has over a long period of time. The climate of far northern lands is cold and snowy for most of the year.

continent (KAHN tuh nuhnt)
A continent is a giant mass of land, such as Africa or North America. There are seven continents, but sometimes Europe and Asia are thought of as one continent called Eurasia (yu RAY zhuh).

descendant (dee SEHN duhnt)
A descendant is a living thing that is born into a group of living things that have the same ancestor. You are a descendant of your parents.

dissolve (dih ZAHLV)
To dissolve means to mix something into a liquid until it becomes part of the liquid. You can dissolve sugar in water.

dromedary (DRAHM uh dehr ee)
The dromedary, or Arabian camel, lives in Arabia, North Africa, and parts of India. It has one hump. The Bactrian (BAK tree uhn) camel of Asia has two humps.

evolve (ee VAHLV)
To evolve is to change from one kind of thing to another over a long, long period of time. Reptiles evolved from amphibians over millions of years.

extinct (eck STIHNKT)
When one kind of living thing dies out completely, it becomes extinct. Dinosaurs are extinct.

fossil (FAHS uhl)
A fossil is the remains of something that was once alive and has been preserved in some way. The bones of prehistoric animals that you see in museums are fossils.

gills (gihlz)
Gills are the part of a water animal's body used for breathing. Fish, lobsters, and other animals that can breathe only in water, breathe with gills.

glacier (GLAY shuhr)
A glacier is an enormous sheet of ice. Glaciers form from snow on mountaintops. They slowly move down the mountainside and may spread out over the land.

guanaco (gwah NAH koh)
A guanaco is a small, wild mammal that lives in South America. It is a member of the camel family, but has no hump.

hemisphere (HEM uh sfihr)
A hemisphere is half of the earth's surface. North and South America are in the Western Hemisphere. Australia is in the Eastern Hemisphere. Countries south of the equator are in the Southern Hemisphere.

lagoon (luh GOON)
A lagoon is a small lake or pond of salty water that is separated from the sea by mounds of sand.

lizard (LIHZ uhrd)
A lizard is one kind of reptile. Most lizards have four legs, but some lizards do not have any legs. Some look almost like snakes and others much like crocodiles.

llama (LAH muh)
The llama is a South American mammal that looks somewhat like a camel, but is smaller and has no hump.

mammal (MAM uhl)
All mammals are warm-blooded animals that are fed milk from the mother's body. All mammals have some hair on their bodies. Cats, dogs, horses, cows, monkeys, whales, dolphins, opossums, platypuses, and people are all mammals. *See also* the words **marsupial, placental mammal,** and **platypus.**

marsupial (mahr SOO pee uhl)
A marsupial is a mammal that carries its babies in a pouch on its stomach. Only a female marsupial has a pouch. Kangaroos, opossums, and koalas are marsupials.

million (MIHL yuhn)
A million is a thousand thousands and is written 1,000,000.

mineral (MIHN uhr uhl)
A mineral is one of the solid materials of which the earth is made. Iron, lead, gold, salt, and diamonds are a few of the many minerals. All rock is made up of minerals.

opinion (uh PIHN yuhn)
An opinion is what a person thinks about something, but does not know for certain. A scientist's opinion of what dinosaurs looked like and how they lived is based upon his knowledge of living animals and what has been learned from fossils.

opossum (uh PAHS uhm)
The opossum, or possum, is a small, furry mammal that lives in both North and South America. It is a marsupial and carries its newborn babies in a pouch. When the babies are about two months old, the mother opossum carries them on her back.

placental mammal (pluh SEHN tuhl MAM uhl)
A placental mammal is one that gives birth to fully formed babies. While the baby is inside the mother's body, it gets food and oxygen from a part of her body that is called the placenta. Dogs, horses, whales, and people are placental mammals.

platypus (PLAT uh puhs)
A platypus is one of only two kinds of mammals (the other is the spiny anteater) that lay eggs instead of giving birth to live babies. The platypus has a furry body, a ducklike bill, and webbed feet. It lives in Australia and Tasmania.

preserve (prih ZERV)
To preserve something is to keep it safe so that it will not be spoiled or damaged. Bones of many prehistoric animals have been preserved because they were safe inside rock for millions of years.

prey (pray)
Prey is any animal hunted by another animal. Rabbits are the prey of wolves. To *prey on* means to hunt or kill another animal for food. Wolves prey on rabbits.

reptile (REHP tuhl)
A reptile is one of a group of animals that are cold-blooded, have scaly skin, and breathe with lungs. Snakes, lizards, turtles, alligators, and the tuatara are reptiles.

scorpion (SKAWR pee uhn)
A scorpion is a small, many-legged animal with a poisonous sting in its tail. It belongs to the same group of animals as the spider.

sediment (SEHD uh muhnt)
Sediment is bits of solid material that settle to the bottom of a liquid. Rivers carry sand to the sea, where it settles to the bottom as sediment. Rock formed from sediment is called sedimentary (sehd uh MEHN tuhr ee) rock. This is the kind of rock in which most fossils are found.

sponge (spuhnj)
A sponge is a water animal that looks like a plant. Fossil sponges have been found in some of the oldest rocks.

streamlined (STREEM lynd)
A streamlined thing has a shape that makes movement through air or water very easy.

tentacle (TEHN tuh kuhl)
Tentacles are long, snakelike arms on the head, or around the mouth of certain animals. An octopus has eight tentacles.

tropical (TRAHP uh kuhl)
Tropical means something in or from the tropics, the hottest part of the world. Palm trees are tropical plants.

Illustration Acknowledgments

The publishers of *Childcraft* gratefully acknowledge the courtesy of the following photographers, agencies, and organizations for illustrations in this volume. When all the illustrations for a sequence of pages are from a single source, the inclusive page numbers are given. In all other instances, the page numbers refer to facing pages, which are considered as a single unit or spread. All illustrations are the exclusive property of the publishers of *Childcraft* unless names are marked with an asterisk (*).

Cover: John Wallner
1: Science Museum of Minnesota*
2,3: Kinuko Craft
8-11: George M. Suyeoka
12-15: Michael Eagle; by permission of the Trustees of The British Museum of Natural History*
16-21: George M. Suyeoka
22,23: Smithsonian Institution*
24,25: Field Museum of Natural History (*World Book* photo); James M. Staples*; Donald Baird*; Donald Baird*
26,27: Bill Ratcliffe*; Donald Baird*; Instructional Media Center of the University of Nebraska*; Bill Ratcliffe*; Bill Ratcliffe*
28-29: Darrell Wiskur; Norman Myers, Bruce Coleman Inc.*
30,31: James Teason
32,33: George M. Suyeoka
34,35: National Park Service*
36,37: Dick Martin
38,39: Kinuko Craft
40,41: Donald Baird*; Rod Ruth
42,43: Rod Ruth
44,45: Jean Helmer; Joe Cellini
46,47: Joe Cellini
48,49: Joe Cellini; Runk/Schoenberger from Grant Heilman*; Jean Helmer
50,51: Kinuko Craft
52,53: Kinuko Craft; Donald Baird*
54,55: Michael Eagle
56,57: Hal Harrison, Grant Heilman*; Jean Helmer; Darrell Wiskur
58,59: Jean Helmer
60,61: Darrell Wiskur
62,63: D. R. Schwimmer, Bruce Coleman Inc.*; Peabody Museum of Natural History, Yale University*
64,65: Linda Gist
66,67: Kinuko Craft
68,69: Donald Baird*; Helmut Diller
70,71: Helmut Diller
72,73: Robert Keys; Jane Burton, Bruce Coleman Inc.*; Robert Keys
74,75: James Teason
76,77: Alex Ebel
78-81: Jean Helmer
82,83: Linda Gist
84,85: Kinuko Craft
86,87: Field Museum of Natural History (*Childcraft* photo); Walter Linsenmaier
88,89: Walter Linsenmaier

90,91: Donald Baird*
92,93: Frank M. Carpenter*; Robert Keys
94,95: James Teason
96,97: *Childcraft* photo; Jean Helmer
98,99: Rod Ruth
100,101: Jan Wills
102,103: Michael Eagle
104,105: Jennifer Emry-Perrott
105,107: Linda Gist
108,109: Kinuko Craft
110,111: ©Steve Leonard*; Helmut Diller
112,113: Helmut Diller
114-117: Kinuko Craft
118,119: Jean Helmer
120,121: Doug Wilson, Black Star*; Jean Helmer; James Teason
122-123: Peter Barrett; Richard Orr
124-127: Richard Orr
128,129: ©Steve Leonard*
130,131: Edward Brooks
132,133: Rod Ruth
134,135: Jean Helmer
136,137: Bernard Robinson
138,139: Science Museum of Minnesota*
140,141: James Teason
142-143: Michael Eagle
144-145: Phil Weare; Michael Eagle
146-149: Darrell Wiskur
150,151: Jean Helmer
152,153: Jean Helmer; Len Rue Jr., Bruce Coleman Inc.*
154,155: Science Museum of Minnesota*
156,157: John Francis
158,159: Rod Ruth
160,161: Pictorial Parade*; Jean Helmer
162,163: Steven Adams
164,165: Donald Baird*
166,167: Michael Eagle
168,169: Robert Keys; Smithsonian Institution*
170,171: Alan Blank, Bruce Coleman Inc.*; Jean Helmer
172,173: Steven Adams
174,175: Steven Adams; Robert Keys; Donald Baird*
176,177: Donald Baird*; Robert Keys
178,179: Richard Orr
180-183: Linda Gist
184,185: Kinuko Craft
186,187: Donald Baird*; Walter Linsenmaier
188,189: Walter Linsenmaier
190,191: Leonard Lee Rue III, Bruce Coleman Inc.*; Jean Helmer; Leonard Lee Rue III, Bruce Coleman Inc.*; Quantas Airways*
192,193: Jean Helmer
194,195: Darrell Wiskur
196-199: Richard Orr
200,201: Robert Keys
202,203: Darrell Wiskur
204-207: Jan Wills
208,209: Steven Adams
210,211: Michael Eagle
212,213: Michael Eagle; Bernard Robinson
214-217: Bernard Robinson
218,219: Darrell Wiskur; Jean Helmer; Lloyd A. McCarthy, Tom Stack & Assoc.*
220,221: Steven Adams; Donald Baird*
222,223: Donald Baird*; Darrell Wiskur
224,225: Kinuko Craft; Leonard Lee Rue III., Bruce Coleman Inc.*; Bruce Coleman Inc.*
226,227: Darrell Wiskur
228,229: Robert Keys
230,231: Richard Orr; Donald Baird*
232,233: Kinuko Craft
234,235: Robert Keys
236-239: Linda Gist
240-241: Kinuko Craft

242,243: Donald Baird*; Helmut Diller
244,245: Helmut Diller
246-251: Jan Wills
252,253: Rene Burri, Magnum*; Lascaux (Fotogram from Jeroboam)
254,255: British Museum (Jean Vertut)*; Rouffignac (Jean Vertut)*
256,257: Michael Eagle
258,259: Tass form Sovfoto*
260,261: Linda Gist
262,263: Kinuko Craft
264,265: I. Howard Spivak, DPI*; Richard Rush Studio (*Childcraft* photo)
268-271: Spencer G. Lewis, Brigham Young University*
272,273: John Linton, Orem, Utah*
274,275: D. Baird*; National Museum of Natural Sciences, National Museums of Canada*; Donald Baird*
276,277: Natural History State Museum, Utah*; National Museum of Natural Sciences, National Museums of Canada*; The University of Nebraska, Lincoln*; Smithsonian Institution*
278,279: The University of Nebraska, Lincoln*
280,281: The University of Nebraska, Lincoln*; Michael Collier, Stock, Boston*; Donald Baird*
282,283: © Walt Disney Productions*; William Dobias*; P. Renick, Sculptor (Milt Butterworth)*
284,285: Australian Museum (Gregory Millen)*; *Childcraft* photo
266,287: *Childcraft* photo

Index

This index is an alphabetical list of the important things covered in both words and pictures in this book. The index shows you what page or pages each thing is on. For example, if you want to find out what the book tells about a particular animal, such as the *Archaeopteryx,* look under **Archaeopteryx.** You will find a group of words, called an entry, like this: **Archaeopteryx** (bird), 172-173, *with picture.* This entry tells you that you can read about the *Archaeopteryx* on pages 172-173. The words *with picture* tell you that there is a picture of the *Archaeopteryx* on these pages, too. Sometimes, the book only tells you about a thing and does not show a picture. Then the words *with picture* will not be in the entry. It will look like this: **Camarasaurus** (dinosaur), 130. Sometimes, there is *only* a picture of a thing in the book. Then the word *picture* will appear before the page number, like this: **Palaeophonus** (arachnid), *picture, 72.*

World Book offers a wide range of
educational and reference materials,
including THE WORLD BOOK MEDICAL
ENCYCLOPEDIA: YOUR GUIDE TO
GOOD HEALTH—1,072 pages of concise,
illustrated information important to your
family's health and well-being. For more
information on THE WORLD BOOK
MEDICAL ENCYCLOPEDIA, as well as
our wide selection of educational and
reference books, please write: World Book
Encyclopedia, Inc., P.O. Box 3073,
Evanston, IL 60204-3073.